To Joe,
  The legend — I am
So proud to know
  you!

George Belden
  WHS 1967

The Windham Bombers

The First Half-Century of Small Town Athletic History

By

George A. Belden

Tripnavvy Press
Kent, Ohio

First Edition

Copyright © 2016 George A Belden

ISBN-13: **978-1534646438**

ISBN-10: **1534646434**

To Harold Belden,
who sent me on a multi-year wild goose chase for a mythical *Parade Magazine* to prove that his 1940 six-man Windham football team was the best in America.
They were.
But it was actually an *American Boy Magazine* I was looking for.
Dad, I found it.

Introduction

Windham Ohio is a town so small one has to squint to see it in a Rand McNally atlas. Situated in the Western Reserve of northeastern Ohio, it is a cookie-cutter five mile square, just like every one of its neighboring townships in Portage County. Established in 1811 by 16 families from Becket Massachusetts, it spent its first 150 years as a rural community with a crossroads hamlet at its center. It has a village green flanked by two churches created almost simultaneously by the founders. "Bucolic" pretty much summed it up until World War II.

Windham built its first high school in 1883, and graduated its first class of four scholars in 1886. Because its population never rose above 300 for the first 130 years, the only organized sport at first was community baseball. Sometime after the turn of the twentieth century, the high school began sponsoring football teams on a field across the street from the white, wooden high school located on today's Bauer Avenue. These teams tended to exist or vanish from year to year, and in the lore of Portage County, none of them are remembered as being very good.

The history of Windham athletics changes in 1927 with the construction of a new all-brick high school with the town's first gymnasium, on the site of the former football field. Beginning in that year, Windham had a baseball team, and both boys and girls basketball teams. Boys and girls participated in a county track meet each spring, but there were no formal track teams. Football sponsorship continued to be haphazard during the 1930's as the small high school often did not even have eleven boys enrolled at one time. That would soon change, and Windham became a completely different community after 1940.

But 1927 is where this history will start. It will take the reader through chapters describing the girls basketball teams that rose to the top of their sports. Several chapters follow football teams that win state championships and are proclaimed the best in the world by experts. Boys basketball teams that win numerous conference trophies and sport the best records in the state of Ohio, the football team that become Portage County's first entry in the nascent state football playoffs, Windham's role in the smallest athletic confederation in the history of the state – these are all part of Windham's heritage.

And the longest chapters will dissect the career of the most respected man to ever coach in Portage County, who scaled the heights of success in three different sports.

The book covers 1927 through 1974, roughly the first half-century of interscholastic sports. The Windham Bombers have achieved even more in the subsequent years. The rebirth of girls sports under the guidance of the tireless Frances Davis, the basketball dynasties of Marty Hill, the football playoff teams of Joe Baum, the numerous visits to the Final Four in baseball, the dominance of Bomber volleyball teams coached by Michael Chaffee, the stunning girls basketball success of coach Gregg Isler, the move from the Portage County League to the Portage Trail Conference to the Northeastern Athletic Conference – those triumphs remain to be chronicled in all their glory.

As the late Bombers coach Jeff Stanley was fond of saying, "Every day is a good day to be a Bomber!"

George Belden
February 11, 2016

Girls Basketball, 1927-1940

Windham High School has been blessed with a long line of great basketball coaches – Corwin Gehrig, Dave Thomas, Arch McDonnell, Dick Schlup, Harry Kraft, Bob Jordan, and Marty Hill, probably the best current coach in the state of Ohio. We're actually kind of spoiled here – enjoying the success of each year, and letting past glories recede from our memories.

But the beginning of Windham basketball was a very different time, and our history starts with what was perhaps the greatest of the Windham basketball dynasties – the girls, not boys, but GIRLS, basketball teams of the 1930's.

The story begins in a three story wooden school that once sat at the corner of High Street, today's Bauer Avenue, and School Street, today a lot where the students park their cars. That building was Windham Central School, erected in 1883, and graduating Windham's first four alumni in 1886. Village students could attend this local school for free, but township students who wanted to attend the new Central School had to pay $1 a month tuition. There was no transportation, and all students walked to school, no matter where they were coming from. It was the most modern school in Portage County. And for forty-four years, this was Windham High School.

Gladys Frees, a young girl sitting in a second story classroom one day in 1926, penned this ode to her school:

The school house in its frame of trees
Is white, and has a pointing spire
Which seems to urge each one to seize
The chance to climb to something higher.
Across the streets the goal posts stand
The scene of many a warlike mess.
Search where you will, in every land,
The dearest spot is W. H. S.

Just one year later, the poem would be antiquated, because on October 3, 1927, if Gladys Frees were still sitting in that same classroom, she would no longer see the goal posts across the street. She would see a red brick structure with two tiny pine trees planted in front of it. And attached to the back of that new building, heralding a new era for Windham, was the one amenity that the dear old white building lacked – a gymnasium. No longer were football and baseball the only sports at Windham High School – basketball had come to town.

The gymnasium – which later generations came to know as the Old Gym – was magnificent. There wasn't much in the way of seating in 1927 – bleachers on the south wall were added years later. In fact, there was only room for one row of chairs along the wall. But it was a veritable palace – it actually had showers, which most of the students, lacking indoor plumbing, had never seen before.

For that matter, most of them had never seen a basketball before. Oh, the sport had been around Portage County for years, and female teams had been playing competitively since 1916. Girls from Mantua Village, Mantua Center (which despite the name was actually the township school), and the Garrettsville Red Sox (long before their teams became G-Men) had been terrorizing the county for over a decade.

But football – badly played, judging by Windham's records, but glorious, manly, leather-helmeted football – was the sport the locals loved. And because the football season ran until the end of November, it was the girls who got a head start on learning the sport which remains central to Windham's athletic legacy.

Reconstructing the history of Windham girls basketball is an arduous task for any historian. One has to work from grainy microfilm which is sometimes impossible to read. There were no sports sections, as they are defined today, in the 8 page *Ravenna Republican*, which was the only paper in which Windham sports had any coverage. Box scores were plugged into any available space: on the society page, in the classified ads, even mixed in among comic strips. First names were never given in articles, last names were often misspelled, games were sometimes reported two weeks after they were played, and seldom were articles more than a few sentences. Of course, in a game in which entire quarters went by without a basket, it might have been hard for reporters to find anything to say.

In the fall of 1927, there were only three male faculty members in the entire Windham school system. Irwin B. Bauer was the Superintendent, Dwight Brocklehurst was the manual arts teacher, and Raymond W. Hilty was the principal.

Whether by choice or by lot, Principal Raymond Hilty became the head coach, in fact the ONLY coach, of every single athletic team that Windham High School fielded.

He was the baseball coach in the spring. He was the football coach in the fall. And now, he was the coach of two basketball teams which had never stepped on a basketball court before.

And he taught all the English and social studies classes too.

Now, if a person met Raymond W. Hilty on the street, one might be forgiven for not even noticing him. Standing about 5 foot 4, hair parted in the middle, wearing round glasses that give him a decidedly milquetoast appearance, he resembled the old comedian Wally Cox, known as Mr Peepers on 1950's television. In the faculty pictures, the female teachers towered over him. Early Windham basketball player Bob Ehresman, writing in 1978 to Superintendent Robert Wert, said that he believed Mr Hilty had never played basketball in his life, either in high school or at Bluffton College.

Bob Ehresman was wrong.

In the Allen County Museum in western Ohio sits a program from a 1921 basketball tournament, showing Raymond Hilty, wearing number 84, playing basketball for Pandora High School. Whatever he did athletically in college at Bluffton, in 1927 he was leading Windham into the completely uncharted waters of the Portage County Conference, which at that time consisted of TWENTY different high schools, most of which are long gone through consolidation.

So Ray Hilty decided to learn more about the game. Even though he seldom had any spare time from all his duties, he joined the Windham Village basketball team, and played community basketball around the county every weekend, a tiny forward learning the ins and outs of the game.

Once football season ended, Hilty established a regular schedule which continued for the entire history of Windham girls basketball. The girls would practice on Monday and Wednesday, the boys would practice on Tuesday and Thursday, and on Friday, both teams would play in a doubleheader, the girls game followed by the boys. That meant both teams would be riding on the same bus to games, so Hilty had to add the role of chaperone to his never-ending tasks.

The boys he put in the floor that first year were a rugged lot. Just naming the lads who graduated from Windham, he had Willis Belden, Bob Ehresman, Robert McCullough, Dan Randall, Louie Snyder, Burdette Woods, and Willis Stavenger. Judging by pictures of them from that year, they appeared to have "athlete" written all over them.

On a basketball court, it was a different story for the Windham Yellowjackets, their team name in 1927.

On December 19, the Windham boys proudly stepped onto their new basketball court in their crisp resplendent uniforms to face the mighty Mantua Village team.

In a game of four eight-minute quarters, in a sport in which single digit scores were not unusual, Windham lost their first game, 92-5.

It would be over 50 years before another Portage County basketball team scored that many points. It remains the most lopsided mauling in county history.

The boys improved dramatically in their second game against Garrettsville, losing only 67-9, causing the reporter to note that "The Windham boys battled even though they knew from the start that they had no hope of victory."

The Windham boys basketball team did not win a single game for exactly four years. They lost forty-one games in a row.

And that's why this history focuses on the GIRLS teams.

Because the girls team had that head start in practicing, they were much more competitive in their first game, losing to Mantua Village 26-15. The team had only six players who played well enough to get into the games – the rest of the girls were still learning. Seniors Sylvan Smith and Pauline Newbrander, juniors Daisy Marcella and Dorothy Loomis, sophomore Doll Young, and a young freshman named Gladys Snyder were the heart of Ray Hilty's initial effort.

The girls played the same game as the boys – five on five – but their quarters were only six minutes long. The men who controlled Ohio athletics didn't feel the girls could stand up under the rigors of an eight minute quarter. This patronizing attitude was to grow much, much worse in the decade of the 1930's.

Junior Daisy Marcella established herself as the team scoring leader in the first game with 11 points. She scored another six in the Garrettsville game, even though Windham lost 32-10. In that game, however, the box score shows the name Snyder for the first time, with two points. It was an inauspicious beginning for this blond speedster. Although the youngest player on the team, the coach had appointed freshman Gladys Snyder as team captain. He knew she was special, but Ray Hilty could not have known that fourteen year old Gladys Snyder would become arguably the greatest female athlete in Windham High School history.

Sometimes, if the boys were playing a school that had no female squad, the girls would play a different opponent, so the next week saw a rematch with Garrettsville. That school did not have a gymnasium; its games were played in a church with a court so small the foul circles actually overlapped. But on January 19, 1928, on that miserable floor, the Windham girls won their first game, 16-10. And for the next twelve years, under three coaches, Windham High School became the most feared female team ever seen in the Portage County Conference.

Windham's tenacious defense caused that fear. Doll Young was a ferocious ball hawk. The first of three sisters who would play basketball for Windham, Doll wasn't much of a shooter, but she was fearless in attacking the opponents. Doll was also the epitome of the 1920's flapper generation. A genuine free spirit, she indulged in that most liberated of female activities – she smoked cigarettes. Fortunately, she was also a natural athlete who finished second in the county track meet in the 100 yard dash in 1926, 1927 and 1928. Whether Coach Hilty never knew about the cigarettes, or just didn't want to tangle with the Young clan, he wasn't about to bench his defensive star.

The Yellowjackets finished their inaugural season by winning their last four games. The county tournament was by invitation only, and the directors did not choose Windham as one of the four teams. However, after a third rematch victory over Garrettsville to end the season, the *Ravenna Republican* noted that "this was the last game of the first season for the Windham girls, and it certainly was a proper ending to this first year. Having won four games in succession, this team seems determined to win."

Windham's junior varsity girls' team played its first and only game of the season that night, whipping Garrettsville 32-2. No one knew it at the time, but that was going to be a bad, bad omen for Portage County for years to come.

In the team photo that inaugural year, Coach Ray Hilty is shown proudly sporting a Bluffton College letterman's sweater, so maybe this small, intellectual man knew a great deal more about the game than anyone suspected.

Ray Hilty was a gentle man. Born a Mennonite, he had gone to a Mennonite college, and in Windham had joined the Congregational Church, serving occasionally as lay minister. His wife Betty was active in town organizations. The town loved their superintendent and his children, Mary Elizabeth and Tom. His players loved and respected him, too, because he complimented them on good plays, and had become knowledgeable enough in the sport that when he made a suggestion, they knew it would make them better players.

The fall of 1928 saw a changing of the guard in many areas. The *Ravenna Republican* changed its name to the *Ravenna Evening Record*. Bob Garrett, who would one day become Windham's mayor, assumed the captaincy of the Windham Township basketball team, which played under the name of the Silica Sanders, crushing opponents year after year and winning the county independent championship two years later.

Irwin B. Bauer was no longer Windham's Superintendent – Ray Hilty added that title to his crowded résumé. But Hilty had given up the football reins to Milton Baderstichter, a young man who was the first of several teachers he imported from his alma mater, Pandora High School.

So Hilty had more time to devote to his girls' team, while his boys were still on the gridiron. He had his three best players, scorers Daisy Marcella and Gladys Snyder and defensive bulldog Doll Young, returning. The Fenstermaker sisters, Erma and Thelma, both seniors, and cousins to Gladys Snyder, joined the squad, and two juniors moved up from the JV team – Frances Thomas and center Esther Smith.

Esther Smith was a tall, powerful athlete. The previous spring, she had set a county track meet record in the baseball throw with a toss of 182 feet. The next spring she was to annihilate that record with a throw of 191 feet. Coach Hilty knew he had a strong pivot player around whom to build his offense.

So, with expectations high, they opened the 1928 season against Garrettsville – and lost, 43-13.

What happened? The reason wasn't in the box scores – it was found in the society pages, where it was reported that a wave of influenza had swept the tiny town that week. The girls were so sick they frequently fled to the lavatory during the game, without even calling time out.

So the rest of the league could not suspect that Coach Ray Hilty had built a squad which would not lose another regular season game that year.

Senior Daisy Marcella remained a deadly shooter, and Gladys Snyder, one year older, began to dominate the box scores. Against Paris, Windham won 19-16, and Snyder alone had 15 of those points. It was one of the greatest shooting performances in 1920's Portage County girls' history. J Preston Bloom, the principal and coach of Paris High School, was so impressed that he did not file his usual protest after the game. Bloom, who years later would become a Windham teacher, had a reputation around the county for knowing more about how a game should be officiated than the referee, and frequently saying so in letters to the editor of the *Evening Record*, but his silence after the game was evidence that he had seen a superior team beat his girls.

Meanwhile, Hilty scheduled a boys' game against Ravenna *Junior* High to try to break his losing streak. Windham fell, 26-15, and their misery continued.

Ravenna Township, Aurora, Hiram, and Charlestown fell to Windham's girls. Hilty brought up another defensive player from the junior varsity, a tenacious guard named Lolita Young, sister to Doll, and every bit as liberated. In fact, her yearbook motto would read "Give me a good time, or give me death." Hilty wanted as much depth on his squad as he could muster. He had no intention of being snubbed in the county tournament again.

Because of Windham's string of dominating wins, the conference commissioner was forced to invite them as one of the six-team field at Wills Gymnasium on the Kent State campus. This would be the first time the Yellowjackets had ever played on a full sized court.

As an unseeded team, they had a play-in game against Ravenna Township in the opening round. Gladys Snyder pumped in eight points to go with six from Daisy Marcella, and Windham won its first ever tournament game 21-20. Facing a rematch with early-season foe Paris in the semi-final round for the right to play Garrettsville in the finals, the girls fell prey to defensive jitters and lost 23-17. But Hilty's team was becoming more mature, more experienced, and although Daisy Marcella was graduating, Coach Hilty had a lot left in the tank for the following year.

The 1929-1930 basketball season began under the cloud of Black Thursday, October 24, the day that Wall Street collapsed, beginning a terrible economic downturn that was to drape itself over the next decade. The dreadful Windham football team even canceled its annual game against powerful Garrettsville, fearing that every male athlete in the school would be incapacitated for basketball season.

Then, on November 15, industrial arts teacher Edward Witham, ditching school to go hunting with student Carl Stanley, succeeded in blowing his own foot off with his shotgun, adding one more monstrous problem for Superintendent Hilty just as he was drilling his female hoopsters.

Many of the county schools did not have girls' teams that year, and Windham only had six scheduled games. Opening with a 16-10 loss to Charlestown, followed by a two-week gap in the schedule, did not bode well for Ray Hilty.

But that just gave him time to work harder with the girls. His returners included Gladys Snyder, Esther Smith, Frances Thomas, the Young girls Lolita and Doll, and he had added Beatrice Wood, Dorothy McDivitt, Olga Huhak, Helen Kerns, and a tiny girl named Lois Wilson, the first of three Wilson sisters. Lois, several years later, was to marry a 1927 Windham graduate and baseball player named Huber King, who became famous internationally as one of America's premier woodcarving artists.

Hilty's extra practice time paid off. On January 18, 1930, Paris High School came in for a rematch of the tournament semi-final game of the year before. And junior Gladys Snyder emerged as the first legitimate superstar in Windham athletic history.

Pouring in shots from everywhere on the court, Snyder established a new Portage County girls' scoring record with 26 points. Windham crushed their nemesis from the year before, 45-8. The next week was a 20-19 squeaker over Deerfield. The game the following week, against Aurora, had to be canceled because a smallpox epidemic had broken out in northern Portage County, so Hilty hastily arranged a game against Ravenna Township.

Gladys Snyder remained on fire, netting 16 points, personally outscoring the entire Ravenna Township team in a 28-14 blowout. But coming into town the following Friday was Garrettsville, the defending league champions – a team which had not lost a game in the two years since Windham had beaten them back in 1928.

Garrettsville had not faced Gladys Snyder since that game, and she had no intention of letting the Red Sox streak continue. She came to play that night – and 16 points later had led Windham to a 25-23 dethroning of the champions. Portage County was on notice – Ray Hilty had built an athletic monster. Hiram High School had disbanded its girls' team earlier in the year, so Windham's regular season was over. Just five games were all the preparation the girls had for the 1930 county tournament. Games were scheduled at Wills Gymnasium on a strict schedule – boys' games ran consecutively with girls' games – and each game was allotted just one hour. Since the boys' games might run longer because of overtime, the tournament officials decided that the girls would get the short end of the stick. Windham got to be the team that found out what that meant. There would be no pregame warmups. Windham would meet powerful Mantua Village at 2 PM. If they won, they would play a semi-final at 7:30 PM, and the final game would be the next morning at 10 AM.

So the stage was set for one of the epic battles of Portage County basketball history. Neither Windham or Mantua could gain an advantage. The score seesawed for four quarters, with neither team going up by more than a single basket. And when 24 minutes had elapsed, the scoreboard read 29-29.

The referee immediately pulled a coin out of his pocket and flipped it in the air. Gladys Snyder called heads. It came down tails. Mantua Village moved on to the semi-final, and Windham went home, because the boys needed the court. Though the Yellowjackets had not lost a game since the opening of the season, they rode the bus home, stunned and embittered, but with their heads high. The next morning Deerfield, a team they had defeated earlier in the season, gained the crown as the county champion.

The Windham girls had been cheated out of the chance for a championship by men who had little regard for female athletes. But before the next season ended, the name Windham would be on the lips of every basketball fan in northern Ohio.

Hilty now had more time to work with the girls, because he turned the boys team over to Mr A. E. Geeting, brought in to replace Edward Witham, the unfortunate hunter with only one good foot, as manual arts teacher.

Hilty had kept a remarkable nucleus on the 1930-31 team. Gladys Snyder was now a senior, and returning from the previous year were Lolita Young, Helen Kerns, Dorothy McDivitt, Olga Huhak, Lois Wilson, and Beatrice Wood. Only four new players made the varsity that year: Thelma Phillips, Nathalie Dick, and freshmen Marie Miller and June Millard.

Hilty's players were whip smart. Gladys Snyder was the Homecoming Queen and had a 4.8 grade point average. She would have been the smartest girl in school, except that one little freshman girl had a 5.0. That was Marie Miller, and she had learned to play basketball as well as she answered questions on tests.

It was a good thing that the girls were so smart, because in the fall of 1930, the state of Ohio forced them to learn a new game. The all-male state athletic commission, believing that vigorous play would lead to what they termed "female disorders," at first debated abandoning girls basketball, but instead ordered the adoption of a variation called "six on six."

Besides eliminating the center jump ball after every basket, a sixth player, another guard, was added to the floor. The three forwards stayed on one half of the court, and the three guards were never allowed to go past the center line, so some girls played their entire career without ever taking a shot. Players were allowed only one dribble and then they had to pass the ball. Players could not touch the ball in the possession of an opponent. And if a guard was fouled, one of the forwards, the designated shooter, had to take the foul shot for her. The men in control were satisfied that these rules were necessary to protect the delicate girls from lifelong harm.

None of the girls agreed, but since the alternative was the elimination of the sport entirely, they learned this ponderous new way, played as if the court had been built on the La Brea tar pits.

The 1930-31 season did not start until January 10. Hilty had moved Gladys Snyder to center and designated shooter, and the Yellowjackets stomped Charlestown 43-10, with Snyder canning 20, and her forwards, June Millard and Helen Kerns, both getting 10. But in the next game, with Snyder nursing a cold, she was held scoreless, and Paris avenged their 45-8 whipping of the previous year with a 19-16 win. And next up was Deerfield, the defending league champion.

Back in good health and top form, Snyder scored 14 and Windham gained the win they should have had the year before in the county tournament, topping the Bisons 20-13. And then it was off to the races.

Against Ravenna Township, Snyder had 16 points. Garrettsville came in undefeated, and went home whipped 31-27 as she scored 17. The county had never seen a scoring machine like Gladys Snyder, but then came the inevitable late winter cancellations, disbanded teams, and Windham's blond fury had to cool her heels for two weeks before the county tournament began.

The *Evening Record*'s skimpy preview simply said "Mantua Village is favored to vanquish the upstart Windham maidens." Upstart maidens indeed! Coach Ray Hilty had built his perfect machine, and Mantua Village would have to be at the top of their game when the time came.

Windham opened the tournament on the Kent State campus with a 22-17 win over Randolph. Scarcely having time to catch their breath, the girls took the floor an hour later against their mortal enemy, Garrettsville. The final score was 23-21 in favor of Windham, and Gladys Snyder had set a new tournament scoring record by tossing in 19 of Windham's 23 points.

The stage was set for the championship game the next morning, indeed, as predicted, against the Mantua Village Hilltoppers, featuring Crafts, their left forward who was almost as keen a gunner as Gladys Snyder. The *Speedometer*, the county yearbook, later called this "the greatest girls game in county history." Although Snyder and Crafts were never on the same half of the court at the same time, they watched each other shoot with unerring accuracy. With five seconds left in the game, Dorothy McDivitt heaved a pass downcourt to Snyder, and she calmly launched a shot that never even touched the rim. She had scored 18 points, out-dueled Crafts, and the Windham Yellowjackets had captured the first Portage County championship in any sport in school history.

Snyder and McDivitt were chosen for the All-Tournament team, and Ray Hilty should have gone to bed that night one happy man.

Except he didn't. Coach Hilty had dreams of something more, especially if the state athletic commission followed through on its threats to abolish girls basketball. So the following Monday, from his Superintendent's office, he calmly dialed the Superintendent of Twinsburg City Schools, a much larger school in Summit County.

Twinsburg was the undefeated Summit County champion, and Hilty wanted to challenge them to a game to determine the best team in all of northeastern Ohio.

Nineteen days after their Will Gym triumph, Hilty took his girls to Twinsburg – a longer trip than many of the girls had ever taken before. Twinsburg was ready – they knew they were facing the best female basketball player in northern Ohio in Gladys Snyder. But Hilty had spent two weeks concentrating on the play of his guards, Dorothy McDivitt, Beatrice Wood, Olga Huhak and Lolita Young, and he was MORE than ready.

The Tigers immediately began double teaming Snyder, daring her to shoot. Watson, the high scoring Twinsburg ace, was equally frustrated. The game eventually became a chess match, each team desperately searching for an opening, and 24 minutes later, Snyder had been held to five points, but Helen Kerns and June Millard took up the slack, and tiny Windham High School stood on top of the northern Ohio basketball world, out-dueling Twinsburg 13-12.

The 1931-32 season dawned in the grip of an atmospheric and economic deep freeze. The weather was as cold as the nation's finances, as American began the slide into the depths of the Great Depression. Speculation reigned that Windham was a one-hit wonder now that Gladys Snyder had graduated and headed off to Miami University. Hilty plugged the third of the wild Young sisters, Juanita, into the departed Lolita's position, and added only one other player, Betty Norton. Marie Miller and June Millard, who took Snyder's center position, were happy to have Betty on the team, because now they had a companion to trudge home with them in the dark every frigid night after practice. Betty Norton lived on Horn Road, Marie Miller lived on Route 82, and for the last leg, poor June Millard had to travel though the woods surrounding the Silica Sand quarry, and walk the railroad tracks to her home on Colton Road. It was indeed a different time in those Depression days.

The first two games of the season were canceled by inclement weather, and as Hilty chafed to begin the season, he decided to call Leavittsburg, the defending Trumbull County champions. Although they already had three games under their belt, Leavittsburg agreed to add a non-conference game for both the boys and girls. So on December 12, 1931, Hilty and boys coach A. E. Geeting took their squads on the road for what remains one of the most important events in Windham sports history.

Because, after four years of absolute, teeth-grinding futility, the boys' team won their first game ever, 27-25.

The girls lost 21-20, but Hilty was satisfied; the season was underway, and a new star had emerged on the team, sophomore forward Marie Miller, who led the team with 10 points.

Marie Miller was a spunky lass, but no more so than junior Helen Kerns. They loved each other as teammates, but had an intense rivalry on the court, as each one showcased to be Hilty's designated foul shooter. Every Wednesday they would stay after practice and have a shootout, 10 shots apiece, to see who would earn the honor. Week after week, it was Marie Miller who won. More than once, the next day would see a definite chill in the air whenever Helen passed Marie in the hall. As long as it stayed off the court, Hilty didn't mind, and neither did Marie. Friendship was one thing, but being the designated shooter was another.

The following week, Windham opened their league schedule with Atwater. The boys again won, and for the first time ever, the County boys standings showed Windham sitting at the top. It wouldn't last, but it was nice for the moment.

The girls beat Atwater 32-23, with a well-balanced scoring attack of Miller with 9, Kerns with 12, and Millard with 11. The next week at Paris, Miller climbed to 15 and Kerns had 10 in a 27-12 triumph. The *Evening Record* burst out with an exclamation that "Windham is definitely the class of the league this year."

A tight 21-20 win against Mantua Township followed by a string of canceled games left Windham at the top of the county standings, but tied with perennial powerhouse Mantua Village, which still boasted Crafts as the league's leading scorer. In an otherwise idle week, the girls were elated to hear that Garrettsville had knocked off Mantua, leaving Windham alone on top of the league, despite not playing for two solid weeks. But Garrettsville was coming to Windham next, looking to knock off another contender.

The girls were rusty. Despite jumping out to a 9-0 lead, and Marie Miller pouring in 14 points, the Garrettsville girls triumphed 29-20, leaving the final regular season standings showing a four-way tie between Windham, Mantua Village, Garrettsville, and Rootstown. Because of so many cancellations, the Yellowjackets had the lowest winning percentage among the four.

As the county tournament began, Windham drew Rootstown, a team they had never faced before, and Marie Miller was sick. Hilty quickly added a tall sophomore center, Charlotte Smith, to the team, and moved June Millard to fill Miller's forward slot. In her first game ever on the varsity, Charlotte Smith netted nine points to lead the squad to a 24-18 win. A new star had been born.

The championship game – naturally against the Mantua Village Hilltoppers, the perennial powerhouse – was set for the following week. The newspapers had little room for preview, though, as the nation was gripped with fascination over the kidnapping of aviation hero Charles Lindbergh's baby. Just as the year before, the game was a classic, only this year, it was Mantua Village who came out on top, 26-21, despite Marie Miller outscoring the legendary Crafts by 12 points to 10. And Ray Hilty had Miller, Smith, and Millard for two more years.

The 1932-33 season began in the midst of national euphoria. Franklin Delano Roosevelt had been elected president. Locally, in the midst of tough times, the town had its sparkling girls' team to take its mind off the horrible Depression that Roosevelt had promised to end. Hilty's league runners-up were back intact, and had added seniors Rosalie Isler, Evelyn Turner, Mildred McDivitt, and tall Maxine Stanley, as worthy substitutes.

They opened the season with a win over Garrettsville, and then waited, and waited, and waited to play again. Hilty, frustrated over the cancellations, scrimmaged a brilliant Braceville team twice just to keep his girls active. As the wait stretched to a month, he took his girls to Randolph for a non-conference game, his squad winning 33-22, with his scoring machine of Kerns and Miller tossing in 22 points.

Finally, late in January of 1933, the girls finally saw some league action. Aurora fell to the Windham girls 21-12, and in a win against Deerfield, Hilty gave his reserves some action, putting in Nathalie Dick and Rosalie Isler to feed June Millard, who scored 13. But then the Edinburg Scots disbanded, followed by Hiram, which seemed to be an annual occurrence, and once more the team went three weeks between games. Hilty fretted over the inaction, because Mantua Township was coming to town – not nearly as powerful as the Village team, but no slouches.

He needn't have worried. His players must have gloried to be in action once again, because they literally exploded, setting a new school record for points scored in a 47-33 slugfest. Charlotte Smith had 16, as did Marie Miller, and the girls were still undefeated in the league despite the 21 day layoff.

As the county tournament loomed, Windham and Rootstown were both undefeated, and in a very questionable pairing, were slated to play in the opening game, while Garrettsville and Randolph, each with one loss, played in the other semi-final. Whatever resentment Hilty harbored quickly evaporated as it became apparent early that the Windham girls had nothing to fear in Rootstown. The Rovers fell 21-11, Smith and Miller had 15 points between them, and they were going to face Garrettsville, whom they had defeated in the season opener, in the title game.

Because there was so much local interest, the game was staged on the neutral Mantua Village court. Hilty hated that floor. There was a heated coal stove in one corner, and the Hilltopper girls had long been accused of purposely hip-checking opponents into it and scalding them. But this was Garrettsville they were facing – mortal enemies indeed, but not nearly so adept at hockey-style maneuvers.

Windham was not to be denied. Miller, Smith and Millard combined for 36 points, putting on a spectacular offensive show. But the guards, those lonely, non-shooting guards –Mildred McDivitt, Olga Huhak and Juanita Young – held the Garrettsville girls without a single field goal until late in the fourth quarter, and Windham walked off the floor with its second league championship in three years, 40-11.

Ray Hilty and his players must have been ecstatic, which made what happened next all the more startling.

Ray Hilty announced his retirement.

No one knows what happened, why a coach at the top of his game suddenly left. Windham was growing, and the pressures of education and coaching were colliding. Hilty's time in Windham was winding down. First, he resigned as coach. The next year, he resigned as superintendent, teaching only social studies for a year. And then, Ray and Betty Hilty were gone from Windham forever. The next year, he was the Superintendent at Deerfield Schools, and Windham had a new Superintendent, George Warman, whose father, also a Windham superintendent, had, in 1926, been the only Portage County superintendent ever to die on the job.

There was no scandal – Ray Hilty was as morally upright a man as ever walked the earth – just an unexplainable void that would have to be filled the next year. And while Hilty remained as Superintendent, he made sure his shoes would filled by someone he trusted to take over the best team in the league – A. E. Geeting, the boys' coach.

He could not have found a better replacement. Physically, Geeting actually resembled a taller, balding Ray Hilty, right down to his black framed, round glasses. He taught manual arts and math, and the students loved him. He never failed to help a student in need; he took students to visit colleges, and to Columbus to compete in the State Fair. He wasn't as good at the basketball X's and O's as Hilty, but the league championship team he inherited took him to their hearts.

Happy days heralded the opening of the 1933-34 basketball season. Prohibition had ended four days earlier, and hot dog tycoon Oscar Meyer had the first legal drink in the nation, chugging a pint of beer at four seconds after midnight. Geeting did not have to worry about his players in this regard – though he had to keep a close eye on free-spirited Juanita Young – because they were defending champs, and not about to lose that honor without a fight.

Seven new players joined his veteran squad : Anna Heikkila, a girl who lived south of the railroad tracks, Thelma Thrasher, Lois Wilson's kid sister Dorothy, and Anita Dick, Nathalie's sister. Thelma McManus, Ruth Isler and Arlene Thompson rounded out the new faces.

The Portage County Conference had never seen a force compared to the one Geeting put on the floor that mild winter. Few cancellations stood in the way of a titanic onslaught. After an initial whipping of Garrettsville, in which Charlotte Smith established herself as the league's dominant center with 16 points, the Paris girls were humiliated in a 51-11 whipping, a new Windham scoring record, with Smith scoring 20 and Marie Miller carding 17.

Week after week the league trembled at facing the Yellowjackets. Charlestown fell 35-7, and a first-ever meeting with Streetsboro saw a 36-17 Windham triumph. Miller, Smith and Millard traded scoring leadership, each making sure the other got her shots. When Nelson came to town, Geeting rested his starters, giving Thelma McManus, Arlene Thompson and Ruth Isler their first prolonged floor time.

He even felt so confident that when they visited traditional enemy Mantua Village, he pulled Charlotte Smith to give Anita Dick some experience at center, and still earned an easy 21-4 victory.

Not a single team gave the girls a tough game. Perennial Trumbull County powerhouse Braceville was sent running on the low end of a 22-7 score. As Windham destroyed Mantua Center 35-16 to wrap up their second consecutive undefeated league schedule, the *Evening Record* named Windham as one of the top teams in the state of Ohio.

But the county tournament loomed ahead, and for the first time, every single team was invited to the tournament. There were more games to be played, more chances for upsets, and an undefeated Suffield team waiting. A late February Alberta clipper dropped the temperatures to 16 below zero the week before the tournament, sending a chill through the entire county.

The tournament games were scheduled over three weekends. Opening against Charlestown, the magic threesome of Miller, Smith and Millard each canned seven points in a 21-8 win. But a quirk in the poorly-arranged brackets showed that the next game would be the game that should have been saved for the finals – a match between the two undefeated teams, Windham and Suffield.

As Hilty had done before him, Geeting spent the week preaching defense, and a swarming barrier of Juanita Young, Betty Norton and Maxine Stanley stopped the Redmen cold. Their high-scoring offense was held to two baskets the entire game, Smith and Miller combined for 26 points, and Windham waltzed into the championship game against a Garrettsville team they had defeated easily in the season opener.

The stakes were high. Since both teams had two league championships, the *Evening Record* offered a gorgeous trophy to be be placed in the showcase of the winning squad. Windham was installed as the favorite, and the game was moved to the spacious new gymnasium at Ravenna City High School.

But this time, Geeting made a tactical error. He double-teamed high scoring Mary Jean Bock of Garrettsville, and lightly-regarded, bespectacled Alice Forschner proceeded to run wild, launching 21 points. Garrettsville shut down June Millard with 3 points, and Miller and Smith could not make up the difference. The Yellowjackets fell 31-22, in what the newspaper called the greatest upset in Portage County girls basketball history.

The following 1934-35 season, Geeting had a dilemma. The Wilson family had moved to Nelson, and Dorothy and her athletic sister Violet would be leaving Windham – except that they didn't want to go. This was Dorothy's senior year and they loved playing for Mr. Geeting, so they chose to break up the family instead. Dorothy moved in with Ken and Julia Swigart, Violet moved in with the Hiltys, and the younger siblings went to Nelson. Two years later, Mr. Wilson found himself with a daughter on both the Windham and Nelson teams when they played each other, and the poor man had no idea who to cheer for.

That problem solved, Geeting added a bevy of talent to his team. He lost Marie Miller, but added her sister Marjorie. Nathalie Dick (who went on to sing professionally with the Fred Waring Singers) was gone, but Anita remained. Charlotte Smith and Juanita Young had graduated, but he had several girls to plug in, including Larue Smith, Ruth Richardson, Grace Shively, and two girls with enormous potential, Virginia Nichols, whom everyone called Ginny, and Mighnon Brobst, who was so aggressive that she spent the rest of her career saddled with the nickname Popeye.

The local newspaper, published jointly in Kent and Ravenna, was now tagged with the cumbersome name of "*The Evening Record and Daily Courier-Tribune.*" Martin Davey of Kent was elected governor. Baby Face Nelson was rampaging though the Midwest. The Portage County Conference had become so unwieldy that it was divided into Northern and Southern Divisions. Windham was placed in the Northern Division, with powerhouses Mantua Village, Mantua Township, and Garrettsville.

It didn't matter. After an opening win over Freedom, junior Violet Wilson (whom the newspaper insisted on calling Lilac) became the talk of the league with a 17 point explosion in a victory over Streetsboro. A trip to Southern Division-leading Paris brought home another win, and suddenly everyone was starting to look past all the other opponents to the end of the season, the final game against Garrettsville, which again featured Mary Jean Bock, the league's leading scorer.

However, in one of the cruelest twists of fate in Portage County sports history, Mary Jean Bock, after scoring 28 points against Streetsboro on a Friday night, went to Ravenna the next morning with her boyfriend to buy a new coat. An out-of-work man from Newton Falls chose that morning to steal a purse containing one dollar and fifteen cents from a woman on a Ravenna corner, jump into his car, and run over and kill a teenage girl crossing the street. That girl was Mary Jean Bock

Although an opponent, Bock was well respected by every player in the league. The newspaper called her "the greatest female athlete in Portage County history." All games were canceled the next week in her honor, and although both the boys' and girls' teams from Garrettsville voted to play the season in her memory, there was a hint of sadness in every game the rest of the year.

It would be another month before Windham played again. Shaking off the cobwebs, they rolled over Shalersville, and then played Mantua Township to an 8-8 tie. This time there was no coin flip – the girls just left the court with no winner and no loser, due to the state rule barring overtime for girls.

Another game against Paris brought another win, and then arrived the game with Garrettsville. Without Mary Jean Bock, the game seemed anti-climactic, resulting, ironically, in another tie game, 14-14. It must have been infuriating to simply quit playing, but they had no choice. For the third consecutive year, Windham had gone through the regular season without a loss.

To prepare for the county tournament, Coach Geeting made a fatal decision. The day before their first game, he scheduled a scrimmage against Braceville. He shouldn't have. The girls were tired for their trip to Kent State, and despite 14 points from Mighnon Brobst, Windham fell in the first round, 17-16, to a Shalersville team they had beaten earlier in the season.

... And then Coach Geeting was gone, just as Ray Hilty had left earlier. Geeting left for parts unknown, and Superintendent Warman, the boys coach, faced a decision. He had hired a new teacher, Corwin Gehrig, that year, a young man eager to coach, so Warman turned the boys team over to him, took on the girls' job, and Windham found itself with a superintendent coach once again.

The opening game under Coach Warman was worth inventing a time machine to go back and see. For the first time, a fund-raising game was staged between the varsity and an alumni team. The alumni team had only six members – Gladys Snyder Farrington, now married to the greatest athlete in Garrettsville history, Frosty Farrington; Charlotte Smith, Marie Miller, Ruth Isler, Thelma Phillips, and one of the Young girls. Which one isn't identified, not that it mattered – they were all wildcats on the court. Showing the youngsters that they did not have any sort of diminishing skills, the old timers laid a 37-16 whipping on the varsity.

The girls had a long time to smart over that drubbing, because it would be five weeks before their next game. Freedom, Streetsboro, and Hiram, the boys' opponents, had no girls' teams, and the layoff must have seemed interminable. Finally, on January 18, 1936, they got to face Mantua Village, and although they lost 23-21, the Brobst-McManus pairing scored all 21 points.

And then one of the most bizarre events in Windham High School history occurred. On the night of January 22, 1936, an amazing exhibition basketball team called the Waterloo Wonders was appearing at Wills Gymnasium on the Kent State campus. Coach Gehrig took four of his boys to the game, but on the way back, in sub-zero temperatures, his car radiator froze between Freedom and Ravenna. Gehrig and the boys set out to find a telephone, but somehow Cyrus Smith, junior star of the team (and boyfriend of Ginny Nichols, of the girls' team), got lost. According to headlines blared from the newspaper, a county wide manhunt began for the lost teenager. The next morning, Cy Smith was found in a home on Freedom Street in Ravenna, where a woman who had seen him wandering in the dark had taken him in, nearly dead from the cold. Smith was taken to the hospital with frozen ears, and missed the next game, which the boys were forced to win without him. The course of Windham sports and politics would have changed forever if that kindly Freedom Street woman had not found future Windham Mayor Cy Smith that night!

The girls went on to beat Shalersville, and then lose a close match to Mantua Township. Unexpectedly, the state of Ohio issued a ruling that girls and boys could no longer compete in tournaments together. Windham's tournament date was February 8, and they had no more scheduled games before then. So an ill-prepared Windham squad lost to Ravenna Township 11-10 in the opening round, and Coach Warman's first season came to an unceremonious end.

Warman faced a rebuilding year in 1936-1937, but he had plenty of returning veterans, and added several JV's – Iris McDivitt, Emerett Rose, Virginia Dick, Mary Schwenk, Grace Drumheller, Kathryn McDivitt, and a moon-faced freshman named Charlotte Thrasher.

The boys and girls both opened the season with easy wins over Nelson, whom the girls once again held to only three points. The boys then knocked off Freedom while the girls sat at home, preparing to face a potent Paris High School team which had just destroyed Deerfield 51-10. The boys' team, featuring Earl Stanley, Cy Smith, Bud McDivitt and Ray McDaniel, did not have to play Paris, and they were glad of it. The Paris boys team had the leading scorer in the league, talented Jim Purdy, and the girls team had a nasty defender, Purdy's girlfriend, Katherine Kainrad, whose aggressive play had earned her the nickname Two-Quarter Kate, since she usually fouled out by halftime.

But Warman had his girls ready. Larue Smith, Iris McDivitt and Charlotte Thrasher throttled the high-powered Paris offense, and Windham returned with a 16-10 victory. Next up for both boys and girls would be Mantua Village, always a grudge match, and this would not be an exception.

The girls' game ended in an 18-18 tie, and as always, they had to walk off the court wanting to strangle the men who controlled their sport.

And then the boys game was also tied 18-18 at the end of regulation. As if tensions weren't already ratcheted up, the rookie Mantua coach said the overtime should be sudden death, which was the way the state tournament was played. Coach Gehrig insisted that in Portage County, a complete overtime period was played. Neither coach would budge, and suddenly ties were being loosened, coats were flung off, and the two coaches squared off to settle it with a fist fight! Fortunately, the veteran official ruled in favor of the entire overtime period, and both coaches retired with their faces intact. One single foul shot in the period settled the matter, and Windham returned home with a well-earned victory.

With that, the Windham juggernaut, boys and girls, began steamrolling every team in the county.

Shalersville fell first. Mantua Township was next. The girls had a 13-13 tie, but the boys kicked things into high gear with a 48-11 mashing of Mantua, a prelude to a 46-10 dismantling of Aurora.

Meanwhile, the undefeated girls entered county tournament competition. Facing Ravenna Township in the first game, Brobst and McManus combined for all 21 points in a 21-11 victory, setting up a grudge match with Mantua Township to settle that tie game earlier in the season. Squaring off on the Ravenna High School court in front of a screaming sellout crowd of over 500 people, Coach Warman surprised everyone by starting senior Marjorie Miller for the first time. Seizing her chance, Marjorie tossed in eight points in a defensive struggle to give the Yellowjackets a 12-7 victory.

The next tournament game, against Garrettsville, was a week off, but there was one final league game to be played – against Garrettsville itself! Once again, Warman put Marjorie Miller on the court, and once again she came through for her coach, exploding for 11 points in a 19-5 victory, setting up a classic rematch two days later. Both teams were in top condition, the defenses were magnificent, and again, it was unlikely star Marjorie Miller, who had waited four years for her chance, who made the difference, canning seven points in Windham's 13-11 nailbiter.

Of course, it wouldn't be a Windham-Garrettsville game without controversy. The Garrettsville fans claimed that the *Evening Record* photographer, Bob Merwin, had snapped a flashbulb just as Ruth Harris, the star Garrettsville forward, had prepared to launch a short bunny shot which would have tied the game. They stormed the court, intent on performing violent bodily harm to the rookie reporter, fresh out of Hiram College. Ravenna school officials had to rescue him from the mob.

The next day, editor A. R. Sicuro ran the picture that Merwin had taken – a picture that clearly showed that the ball had already left Harris's hands in a lopsided fashion, exonerating the photographer, but establishing years of bad blood between the two towns.

No matter. Windham had advanced to the championship game against Paris, with Katherine Kainrad and her teammates lusting for revenge for their earlier defeat.

If anyone ever deserved the name Cinderella, it was Marjorie Miller, who brushed aside every attempt to stop her in her very last game. Scoring nine points, she fought tooth and nail to lead her teammates to an epic 15-12 victory. The Windham girls claimed their third league championship in seven years.

The next day Oliver Wolcott, the sports editor of the Ravenna-Kent paper, wrote that he hated girls basketball, even claiming that he would rather watch ping-pong, but that he had never seen such an exciting athletic event as that Paris-Windham girls' game. The Windham fire department dispatched a truck to lead the team bus back to the village. One week later, the community gave the girls an oyster dinner – the highest form of edible praise in the depths of the Depression. This was as good as it would ever get for Windham's female athletes.

The 1937-1938 season looked great for Windham. The year before, the boys had made it to sectionals before losing to eventual state champion Waynesburg, and they had added Fred Stanley to join his brother Earl on the varsity. The girls returned powerful Mighnon Brobst, moved Charlotte Thrasher to forward, and added only three players, Dorothy Hoffman, Lela Bright, and Frances Beckenbach.

But nothing had changed, really. One after another, teams faced the black and gold clad ladies and went away thrashed. Nelson, Ravenna Township, Deerfield – and then came Mantua Village, whom Windham had tied the year before. But this year was different. For the first time in over two years, the girls could not quite pull out the miracle comeback, losing 23-21. It would be their only regular season loss that year.

Sophomore Charlotte Thrasher began to emerge as one of the league stars, but overall team scoring was down dramatically. Opponents ganged up on Mighnon Brobst. The wins came harder, as evidenced by a miserable 9-7 win over Paris that seemed more in tune with the 1920's than the late 1930's.

Still, they finished with the best record in the Portage County Conference, and were pre-tournament picks to win it all. Mighnon Brobst regained her shooting eye in a 15-4 opening win over Ravenna Township, and as usual, Garrettsville loomed on the horizon as the next hurdle.

Garrettsville would be the eventual league champion, because Coach Warman could not come up with a counter for Cooper, the league's leading scorer, and Windham fell 20-12, not even making it to the championship game. The boys then lost in the first round of the tournament, wasting a regular season that also had only one loss. Both teams were good – just not good enough.

And Mighnon Brobst was now gone. Charlotte Thrasher would have to saddle the 1938-1939 team on her back. Ace defenders Grace Drumheller and Iris McDivitt were gone too. New faces included Grace Hoffman, Hazel Lutz, Margaret Norton, and a spunky little freshman named Hazel Schwenk, Mary's sister, who gave an instant energy boost whenever she appeared on the court.

But the big news was no longer girls basketball. There was a new sport in town. Windham had adopted a brand new game called six-man football, and while 1938 was a learning year, that team was soon to overshadow everything in Windham sports history, because within two years they would be proclaimed the greatest team in the United States and Canada.

But that story will have to wait for the next chapter.

Back to the girls. The state athletic association was again making noises about abolishing the sport. Already, 400 high schools in Ohio had dropped the game. Despite the enthusiasm of the players, it already felt like the coffin was closing.

A mumps epidemic ravaged schools, causing cancellations. A rabies outbreak terrified parents around the county. Windham managed a single game in the midst of this, a 21-15 win over Nelson highlighted by a singular occurrence. Guard Mary Schwenk fired a long pass three-quarters of the length of the court, so powerfully thrown that it clanged off the fan-shaped metal backboard and accidentally went through the basket. Referee Tom Mariana had to stop the game and consult the rulebook, as this had never happened in a girls' game before.

Wins over Paris and Garrettsville brightened prospects considerably, but Mantua Village had spawned yet another Crafts girl, Virginia, and she was destroying defenses around the league. Reporter Oliver Wolcott wrote that she was better than anyone in the league, and he meant female OR male. When Windham and Mantua tangled, it was ugly. 33-11 ugly, the worst defeat in the history of the Windham girls basketball program.

Two weeks later, the team recovered its composure with a win over Mantua Township, but the starch was gone. On February 11, the state of Ohio decreed that there could be no girls' tournaments anywhere that year. Portage County Conference officials boldly decided to defy the edict, because the girls' tournaments drew more attendance than the boys', and even though the country was coming out of the Depression, they needed every dime they could generate in revenue.

In the face of such doom and gloom, it came as no surprise when Coach Warman found out that they would face Virginia Crafts and Mantua Village in the first round of the tournaments. Despite Windham losing only a single regular season game, the result was almost preordained. So it was quite a surprise when Warman assigned Mary Schwenk to dog every step that Crafts took. In her final game, Schwenk held the scoring machine to seven points, keeping the final score a much more respectable 17-12.

When the state announced in the fall of 1939 that the sport would be abolished statewide after that season, much worse things overshadowed it. Hitler's air force was making preliminary forays over London, Russia was dropping bombs on Finland, and the government had mysteriously begun buying up land south of the railroad tracks in Windham, forcing families to move out in a matter of weeks. Hazel Lutz disappeared from the team for that reason. So no one gave much of a care for a bunch of girls who were soon to be abandoned.

Coach Warman gave it the old college try. He still had Charlotte Thrasher, Hazel Schwenk, Margaret Norton and Frances Beckenbach, and he added lanky Emily Grodenski, who was soon to become displaced by the future Ravenna Arsenal herself. He recruited junior Iona Chaffee, sophomore Corrine Comyns, freshmen Beulah Smith and Joyce Janacek, and sallied forth into the Portage County wars for the final time.

It was a difficult time for the team that used to battle Mantua Village and Garrettsville in games worthy of the legends. They lost their opener to lowly Nelson, then the following week to Braceville. Warhorse Paris came to town early in January, and the girls showed some spark of the old grit with a 16-9 win.

But there were more losses than wins that year. Occasionally, the fires would return, as when Charlotte Thrasher erupted for 18 points against Shalersville on a night when it was 12 degrees below zero outside. Or when Beulah Smith scored all 10 points that Windham recorded in their only game ever against Newton Falls. Or even when they entered the county tournament, having won only two games all year, and bumped off Ravenna Township 20-11.

That would be the last time a Windham girls' team won a basketball game for 33 years.

Twelve years earlier, the first Windham game was played against Mantua Village. Thus, it was only fitting that the curtain came down against Mantua Village and the brilliant Virginia Crafts. As he had the year before, Warman assigned a Schwenk to guard her, this time the feisty sophomore Hazel. If Windham was going down, Crafts was going to work for her win, and Hazel made sure she did. Crafts paid her back with her elbows, breaking her nose and giving her two black eyes to wear for the next few weeks.

The boys' team was still playing – in fact, would go on that year to win the first boys basketball title in Windham history, under new coach Dave Thomas – and since the girls would never play again, the taller girls were ordered to hand over their warmup jackets to the JV boys, a disgraceful ending to a proud tradition. Hazel Schwenk defiantly refused to wash the blood from her broken nose from her jacket. Two years later, principal Deane Eberwine gave her the uniform she had worn in that last battle with Virginia Crafts, and she treasured it until the day it fell apart in tatters, the last emblem of a glorious past that too soon was forgotten by everyone except the girls who had proudly worn the black and gold.

And Raymond Hilty, the principal who started it all? Mr. Hilty became an ordained minister, moved to Dayton and founded the Greenmont-Oak Park Community Church, affiliated with the United Church of Christ. He continued being their gentle guide and leader until he passed away at the age of 84.

Four players on those teams have been inducted into the Windham Athletic Hall of Fame, along with Coach Ray Hilty: Gladys Snyder Farrington, Charlotte Thrasher McDivitt, Marie Miller Dutter and June Millard Brobst. There are others, such as Charlotte Smith Isler and Mighnon Brobst, who deserve the honor.

Over the course of their 12 year history, these girls won 75% of their games. They loved their sport, they loved their school, but it took an act of the United State government, called Title IX, to restore girls basketball to Windham in 1973. There were so many lost generations of girls who did not get a chance to prove that they could compete on the same floor as the boys. They could be Rosie the Riveter, but they could not legally play basketball.

Every girl who wears the black and gold for Windham High School, today and forever, walks in the footsteps of these forgotten women.

Six-Man Football – 1938-1940

The 1930's weren't very good years for America's economy, and they weren't much better for Windham High School's football teams. Completely dominated by the much larger county schools, Windham lost every single game in 1936, and Ray McDaniel was the only player deemed worthy of even a mention in the All-County selections.

So, doing the same thing they had done in 1932, the school administration decided to focus on the sports at which Windham **was** good, basketball and baseball, and football was unceremoniously dumped. The *Ravenna Evening Record* reported that Windham even gave away their football equipment, and Windham football players were reduced to playing weekend pickup games with boys from surrounding towns.

But a wind was blowing out of the state of Nebraska, a sirocco which would soon sweep Windham's forlorn gridders literally to the top of the gridiron world.

In the spring of 1934, Stephen Epler, the physical education teacher at Chester High School in Nebraska, not much bigger than Windham and also without a football team, convinced his superintendent to allow him to streamline the game of eleven-man football into a sport which would cost less, allow smaller boys to play, and at which schools with tiny enrollments could compete.

Epler devised a brand of football with fewer rules (nine, to be exact), but with just as much contact and a lot more excitement. He eliminated the positions of guard and tackle and one halfback slot, bringing the number of players from eleven down to six, putting three men on the line, and three in the backfield. He reduced the size of the field from 100 yards by 50 yards to 80 yards long and 40 yards wide.

Although the minimal helmets and padding of the day were retained, shoes with cleats were banned, and the players wore simple canvas basketball shoes, known then and now as Chuck Taylors, which most of them already owned. This one rule dramatically reduced the number of potential injuries in the sport.

But it was in the rules governing ball movement that Epler was completely revolutionary. The most stunning, and actually most simple, rule was that every single one of the six players was eligible to receive a forward pass. No longer were the chubby kids relegated to smashing each other at the line of scrimmage and then falling down – after blocking his man, a lineman could run downfield and have the chance to be the hero who caught the game-winning touchdown, and have all the girls hanging on **him** the next day!

The few other rule specifications were intended to make the action more lively. The player who took the snap from center had to pass or lateral the ball to a teammate before the ball could cross the line of scrimmage. So the position held by the modern quarterback, the field general of the team, would actually have been the **third** man to touch the ball on any play. That one simple rule meant reverses, end arounds, trick plays, and quickness were the norm, not straight ahead line smashes and power.

15 yards in four downs, four points for a drop-kicked field goal, two points for a kicked extra point versus one for running the ball, ten minute quarters – these few basic rules created an entirely new sport which was much more wide open for the players and visually exciting for the fans.

Epler added one more unique rule. If a team was ahead by 45 points at any time after the last second of the first half, the game was over. That's the "mercy" rule; the losing team had the ignominy of being "forty-fived," and Windham was to become the master of imposing it.

After the very first game, played in Hebron Nebraska on September 26, 1934, Stephen Epler's new game exploded across the country as small school coaches and administrators heard about it. By the fall of 1937, it was estimated that four thousand schools had adopted the game, and *American Boy Magazine*, the leading youth magazine of the day, became its champion. Its September 1937 issue featured a gorgeous artistic portrayal of a leather-helmeted runner crashing through a compact defensive line.

Three years after the creation of the sport, on September 25, 1937, Edinburg and Nelson played the first Portage County six-man game at the Randolph Fair, with Edinburg winning 34-0 in front of a large crowd.

Part of that crowd was Windham basketball coach Corwin Gehrig. Gehrig's basketball team had gone nine and one the previous year; he knew he had a nucleus of good athletes, several of whom had the last name of Stanley, and it didn't take much for him to convince Superintendent George Warman that this was the sport for Windham.

And so it began. That initial 1938 season, with the Yellowjackets featuring that slew of Stanleys and Ralph "Nip" Drumheller, opened with Windham crushing Charlestown 59-0 in the first game for both teams. Played on September 23, 1938, on a field behind the Windham village green, the game that was over at the halftime. The *Ravenna Record* took notice, calling Windham "one of the classiest outfits in the county." The next two weeks Windham battled Nelson and Edinburg, two of the veteran teams, to scoreless ties, almost an impossibility in such a wide-open game. Although Windham eventually lost to league champion Mantua Village, they had put Portage County on warning, and Earl Stanley was chosen to the first ever six-man All-Star team.

The 1939 season saw a new mentor of the Windham program. Deane Eberwine, a former eleven-man football center who had graduated from Windham High School in 1920, had returned as an English teacher (and later principal) and he took the football coaching reins from Corwin Gehrig, who left Windham, turning his basketball coaching job over to Dave Thomas. Earl Stanley had graduated, but Eberwine still had Fred and Harold Stanley and Nip Drumheller, along with agile newcomer Bob Turner, center George Love and end Kenny Nichols.

Eberwine jumped eagerly into the coaching fray. Since Windham had a bye the first week of the season due to an odd number of league teams, he arranged scrimmages against Twinsburg and North Jackson, one of Ohio's top teams from 1938. After North Jackson showed his team's weaknesses, Eberwine had one week to retrench, retool, and recalibrate the squad to face defending league champion Mantua Village in the opening game.

With Nip Drumheller scoring three touchdowns, Windham knocked off this powerhouse 26-14, launching a run of victories which arguably ranks as the greatest two-year streak in the history of Ohio sports.

Week after week Portage County foes dreaded the sight of the black and gold clad Windham squad. The Deerfield Bisons fell 49-0, with six different Windham players scoring touchdowns. Mantua Township lost by an identical 49-0 score, with Harold Stanley scoring four times. Charlestown managed a single score in their 42-6 drubbing, and by this time the *Ravenna Record* was calling Windham "one of the leading teams in all of Ohio", which actually was one of the few examples of understatement in 1930's sports writing.

On October 26, 1939, Windham defeated Shalersville 1-0. That's what it says in the record books. But the reality is that Shalersville coach George Converse refused to allow his players to come back on the field for the second half, actually fearing for their physical safety. So the 32 points Windham had scored officially disappeared, but Hiram, Edinburg and Nelson, the remaining opponents, knew exactly what was in store for them.

Hiram gave Windham its best game of the season, falling 19-6, and the newspaper was abuzz all week with articles about the coming showdown with undefeated Edinburg.

The score of that game was 33-0.

Oliver Wolcott, the legendary Ravenna sportswriter, wrote: "With that decisive victory over the Scots, the <u>Bombers</u> team established itself as a possible contender for the Horlick Trophy [sponsored by a malted milk company], given annually to the outstanding team in the country."

That quotation, from the fall of 1939, is perhaps the most important single collection of syllables in Windham High School history. *Because with one line of type, Wolcott, who had been enthusing over passer Bob Turner's ability to "bomb" opponents with his unerring throws, had given Windham High School athletes, known informally as the Yellowjackets for a decade, the name they would carry in perpetuity. From that day forward, they would be the **Bombers**, a name bestowed long before the Ravenna Arsenal was created.*

In the last game of the season, Windham beat Nelson 37-0, and Ralph Drumheller, the only senior on the Bombers squad, became Windham's first ever County scoring champion. Nip, Harold Stanley and Fred Stanley were chosen to play in the Portage County eleven-man All-Star game on Thanksgiving Day, in spite of the fact that not one of them had ever played the eleven-man version of the game, and Drumheller even got his picture in the paper for a play in that game.

Oliver Wolcott wrote an editorial campaigning for a state championship game between Windham and Huron High School, also undefeated, but since basketball season was only a week away, this clash of the titans never happened.

The 1939 Windham team, with only 10 players on the squad, was 8 and 0, had outscored their opponents 281-26 despite having "forty-fived" three opponents, and recorded an unbelievable five shutouts. In the February 1940 issue of *American Boy Magazine,* Stephen Epler, the man who had created the sport and awarded the Horlick Trophy, chose Windham as the Number 16 team in the United States, calling them "a powerful team with an impregnable defense." *American Boy* awarded Windham a "small" Horlick Trophy and $15 in athletic equipment, an absurd figure today, but back then enough to buy canvas shoes for the entire squad.

Huron High School, the next highest Ohio selection, was number 23, effectively making the Bombers the 1939 Ohio State champions. Bob Turner, whose massive hands enable him to deftly pass the oversized, rugby-styled ball to the Stanley boys and Drumheller, was selected to Epler's All-American team, and the *Ravenna Record* published a picture of him receiving the Horlick Trophy and his All-American commendation from Coach Eberwine.

All of this was just a prelude to greatest team of all.

On September 7, 1940, Hitler began the massive blitzkrieg of London, and eight days later the United States Military Conscription Act was passed, casting a pall over the young football players who assembled for Coach Eberwine, especially center Robert Fechter and Fred Stanley, the only seniors.

But when Windham opened the season against Twinsburg, it was as if 1939 had never ended. Sam Scott, who had seen considerable backup action the year before, erupted for 30 points as the Bombers thrashed the hapless Tigers 51-6.

The next week saw Shalersville fall by the magic number of 45-0, just as 51 minus 6 the week before had equaled 45 and a mercy conclusion. In the Shalersville game, after Fred and Harold Stanley had scored 2 quick touchdowns apiece, Eberwine pulled them off the field to try to keep the score under 45 so his substitutes could get some action, but Con Thrasher, Frank Janecek and Sam Scott all scored in quick succession to foil the coach's plan.

This scoring explosion launched sports writer Oliver Wolcott, who never met an adjective he didn't like, into a rhapsodic flight of superlatives. "This Windham team," he wrote, "is so well drilled and impressive that each week is nothing more than a practice game against the type of opposition offered by other county six-man teams. Perhaps their domination of six-man football will come to an end in the next few years, yet it is unlikely, because coach Deane Eberwine has thoroughly stressed the importance of fundamentals. Few persons who witness the Bombers in action cannot help but be impressed by the precision performance of the squad. In fact, supporters of six-man football are now crying for a game between Windham and the eleven-man champions. These enthusiasts are willing to pit Windham against any team in the state, playing one half of the game according to the eleven-man rules and the other half by six-man rules."

The third game of the season was a carbon copy of the first two, as Mantua Township held the Bombers to a scant 25 points in the first half. Any hope of staving off the executioner faded fast, though, as Windham punched in 22 points in five minutes of the third to once again invoke the mercy rule.

The next week was a different story. Upcoming was a showdown with the undefeated Hiram Huskies on the following Tuesday, only four days after the Mantua Township game. Oliver Wolcott breathlessly reported that "Coach Deane Eberwine was fighting overconfidence on his squad and went so far as to predict a defeat for his high scoring aggregation."

Reverse psychology must have worked, because the next-day headline for that Hiram game reads: "Harold Stanley leads way, scoring three touchdowns: Hiram is first team to hold Bombers under 45 points in 40-12 loss." The Huskies, apparently, had to be content with moral victories.

But Eberwine was still happy – his boys had gotten as much playing time in that game as in the first three games combined. They needed it, because Eberwine, no slouch when it came to seeking a bit of notoriety for his squad, had decided to schedule a non-conference game for the fifth match of the season.

Eberwine had let his imagination run wild, and had arranged a road game against the undefeated and likely champions of the entire country of Canada – the first game ever scheduled between teams from that country and the United States.

He knew that would get Stephen Epler's attention at *American Boy Magazine*. He had no intention of Windham finishing 16th in the Horlick Trophy balloting again.

Eberwine furiously worked the newspapers that first week of October in 1940. He told the *Cleveland Press*, "Our boys are pretty good. We're not as big as them, since our weights run from 123 (that being tiny sophomore reserve Don Miller) to 170 pounds, but where our boys excel is in their ability to handle the ball."

Photographers from the national Associated Press came to practice to take pictures of the starters: Bob Turner, Fred Stanley, Harold Stanley, Frank Janecek, and two juniors who had recently become starters, halfback Joe Pinney, and, squatting down in the middle of the line, assuming the position that every member of his family was doomed to follow, center Harold Belden.

Only 60 hours after the conclusion of the game with Hiram, the Windham Bombers packed their thin pads, leather and cardboard helmets, dirty uniforms, and 11 players, almost a third of the school's male enrollment, some of whom had never been beyond the borders of Portage County, piled into several automobiles and set off in a caravan for Niagara Falls Canada, and their meeting with powerful Stamford Collegiate at Oakes Stadium on Saturday, October 5, 1940.

Also making that trip were the Windham cheerleaders, Iona Chaffee, Wanda McManus, Margaret Norton and Belvera Smith, who recalled that the girls had to dress their best, down to stockings and hats, and were guarded like prisoners by teacher Isabel Kennedy before being sent into Oakes Stadium in their black corduroy skirts and gold tops with puffy sleeves.

Fred Stanley remembered that they stayed overnight as guests in the homes of Stamford players. Don Miller, in 1990, said the trip was fun, but that as soon as he saw the much larger Canadians, his first thought was, "Uh-oh, we've had it"! Bob Goss, later in life, said that one of the big regrets of his life is that he couldn't be spared at home to make that trip.

The game was played on a nasty day, using a strange hybrid of American six-man and Canadian Rugby rules, but Coach Eberwine got what he had bargained for – three football games in a seven day span, excitement for his boys, an act of friendship between two countries, and a 39-1 victory to flaunt to Stephen Epler and *American Boy Magazine*.

The *Ravenna Record* headlined the game report: "Windham lays claim to World 6 man grid title." The Niagara Falls newspaper was equally as eloquent: "Windham is the highly touted state grid champions of Ohio. The Bombers backfield gave one of the prettiest displays of running and maneuvering that has been seen in interscholastic football in many a day. Their continuous penetration of the Stamford line, their masterful defense, and their sensational end running galvanized the crowd that braved the weather to see our stalwarts go down to defeat."

And then it was back to the Portage County wars.

Eberwine gave most of his starters the next game off, but the second string proved just as devastating, destroying Nelson 32-0. The layoff for the starters then stretched to two weeks, as Principal M. I. Johnson of Mantua Village High School called Eberwine and begged him not to bring his team to Mantua, declaring that to allow his players to face the Bombers was tantamount to forfeiting Mantua's entire *basketball* season.

This then left one remaining game, against undefeated Charlestown, featuring Dave King, the league's top scorer, for the Portage County six-man championship. Eberwine and Charlestown principal Howard Cook decided a neutral field was best, so Mantua Village's field, having been unused due to the forfeit the week before, was selected, and they asked Joe Begala, the former head football and then current wrestling coach at Kent State University, to referee what was expected to be a real donnybrook.

And then disaster struck. Two days before the game, team stalwart Frank Janecek was taken from school with an attack of acute appendicitis. Eberwine's choice to replace him, little used George Brauker, announced the next day that his family was moving to Cleveland. And Sam Scott, who had been a two-year mainstay, had unexpectedly withdrawn from school to join the Marines. The Stanley boys could still be expected to shoulder most of the load, but suddenly a skinny junior, Joe Pinney, found himself the focus of a great deal of Eberwine's attention.

Fortunately, Frank Janecek was not planning to stay in his sickbed. He declared that he felt well enough to play, and on Friday suited up for the game with his teammates in Mantua. And vaunted Charlestown? They gave up 33 points in the first 15 minutes, barely staving off the mercy rule with three late scores after the reserves entered the game, leaving the final score 45-18. Eberwine even inserted the team manager, senior Robert Pavlik, into the game!

A bunch of lightweight 16 and 17 year old farm boys had done the unimaginable, week after week, for two consecutive years, winning both Portage County Championships, the 1939 Ohio state championship, and the first game ever played between two countries.

All that was left was to wait for the February 1941 issue of *American Boy*. And when it arrived in the mail, the first sentence of the article read, "This year, the *American Boy* is not publishing an All-American six-man football honor roll." Apparently the task of collating 4000 teams had overwhelmed the editors, and Coach Deane Eberwine was one year too late.

However, the next paragraph stated: "Here are the teams who **would** have been eligible had we decided to pick All-Americans". In that list of nine teams, Epler lists "Windham, Ohio, whom we declare this year's **INTERNATIONAL** six-man champions."

On the short list of the best players in the United States are the names Fred Stanley, Harold Stanley, and Robert Turner. Tiny Windham High School had placed three players on the official All-American Six-Man football team.

Thus, even though the 1940 Windham Bombers never won that **national** championship Deane Eberwine so coveted, they became the only declared **international** champions the sport has ever had – and six-man football is still played in several states and Canada to this day.

Windham would go on to win more six-man Portage County championships in 1944 and 1946, as well as eleven-man titles after the enrollment boom occasioned by the creation of the Ravenna Arsenal allowed that sport to return in 1947, piloted by Coach Gordon MacDonald. But there would never be another group of boys like the 1939 and 1940 Bombers. Late in his life, Coach Eberwine said, "They played the game with great skill and enthusiasm. They were a team whose crisp blocking and hard tackling did not have to be seen – it could be heard. Those boys loved the game of football."

They were, as historian Tom Brokaw once noted, the greatest generation. Many of those players went off to war, to Europe, Iwo Jima, Guadalcanal, Guam, and Frank Janecek to the air, piloting single engine P-47 Thunderbolts, providing cover for B-25 Bombers. Yet they all came back alive, many to Windham.

Robert Turner and his center, Harold Belden, were the first to pass away, within a year of each other, Turner in a tractor accident on his ranch in Oregon, Belden of a stroke at the age of 46 after serving as Windham councilman, treasurer and clerk in the town he always loved. Some disappeared from Windham without a trace. One by one they left us, until the last two remained: Bob Goss, who became the starting left end in 1941, played professional baseball, and retired to Florida, and Fred Stanley, who became the postmaster of Newton Falls Ohio.

The three All-Americans on these teams were inducted into the Windham Athletic Hall of Fame for their athletic achievements: Bob Turner, whose aerial talents led to the nickname for every Windham athlete after him, fleet running back Harold Stanley, and rugged end Fred Stanley. Their coach, Deane Eberwine, preceded them as an inductee.

A plaque which Windham was awarded as international champions disappeared during the move into the new high school.

Other than their league championship banners which hang in the Marty Hill Gymnasium, the only reminder of these legendary six-man teams in the trophy case is the 1940 Portage County football championship trophy. Sometime in the past, it was manhandled and broken, and now has a garish new figurine on the top of it, wearing an enormous helmet with a facemask, something at which those true leatherhead players would have laughed.

However, both the 1939 and 1940 teams, almost three-quarters of a century after the days of their athletic glory, were finally accorded the highest honor that Windham High School could bestow. They became the first teams enshrined in the WHS Athletic Hall of Fame.

Not many Portage County residents remember six-man football nowadays, but in Windham, it's a proud legacy. Much like the basketball movie *Hoosiers*, the Windham football teams of 1939 and 1940 were the stuff of which American heartland dreams and legends are made.

Six-Man Football – The War Years

December of 1940 was an unusually cold month in the little town of Windham, Ohio, home to 316 souls and a graduating class of 13 seniors at Windham High School. But one line in a famous magazine had made this little village the toast of the American sports world. *American Boy Magazine* had declared Windham the international champion of the booming sport of six-man football – there was no team in North America better than the Windham Bombers.

They had spent the preceding two seasons demolishing teams in Portage County, with many of their games called at halftime because Windham was leading by more than 45 points. Three of the players on the 1940 team, senior Fred Stanley and juniors Harold Stanley and Bob Turner, had been named first team All-Americans. Coach Deane Eberwine would lose only two players, Fred Stanley and backup center Robert Fechter, from that squad. And he would have to replace his manager, skinny Robert Pavlik, whom he had once substituted into a game in an attempt to keep the score down.

There was no reason to believe that the dynasty would come to an end. Eberwine spent the off-season dreaming of a way to equal his audacity at scheduling a game against the Canadian six-man champions, Stamford Collegiate, in the fall of 1940, and then destroying them 39-1. Yes indeed, it looked like Windham would be an indelible fixture on the sports pages for years to come.

But world history has a strange way of changing things, even in a town as remote as Windham, Ohio.

In 1940, Windham was a 25 square mile township, shaped exactly the same as every other township in the Western Reserve, with a small crossroads village sitting in its center. Using today's road names, the entire village consisted basically of East and West Center Streets from traffic light to traffic light, and North Main Street to its one northern traffic light. But South Main Street, which today ends forlornly at a gate on the other side of the railroad tracks, had a busy commercial section on both side of the tracks, with grocery stores, a post office, and Paul's lumber mill. And for two and a half miles further south were the richest farmlands, and some of the oldest families, in Windham Township.

That is, until August 1940 – because World War II had begun in Europe, and the United States government, knowing full well that America would inevitably be drawn into it, had seized all the land south of the railroad tracks for one of the largest munitions plants in the country. Every person living on that land was evicted, often given less than a week to abandon their family's lands, auction off their goods, and find a home elsewhere. By August 31st, 1940, the largest mass relocation in Ohio history was over.

The entire month of August, as Superintendent Eberwine prepared for the opening of schools, he had to share the high school with government engineers and surveyors who had commandeered classrooms to make preparations for September 1, the first day they could legally enter the seized lands.

The Ravenna Army Ammunition Plant, known locally as the Ravenna Arsenal, became the monster that devoured Windham. Coach Eberwine took his 1940 Bombers to the top of the football world in the shadow of that colossus, and the bucolic little village would never be the same.

On August 18, 1941, exactly three weeks before Coach Deane Eberwine gathered his Windham Bombers to prepare for the defense of their Portage County championship, the first loaded artillery shell rolled off the assembly line in the Arsenal. Those bombs would continue to roll in ever increasing numbers for the next six years. No one knew, at the time, that those assembly lines would one day spell the end of six-man football at Windham High School.

<u>Superintendent</u> Deane Eberwine had spent a hectic year keeping up with the drama of having students who had spent their entire lives in the Windham schools disappearing from the enrollment lists overnight. <u>Coach</u> Deane Eberwine, however, was able to relax, since none of his returning lettermen lived south of the tracks.

On September 10, 1941, the Bombers dedicated their new football field, with one end abutting what is now Bauer Avenue and the other extending towards Charlie Curtis's cow barn, only a dropkick away from the Arsenal fence that now cut Windham in half. At the dedication, Eberwine was presented with a bronze plaque honoring Windham's international victory over Stamford Collegiate of Niagara Falls, Canada. And he announced to the crowd the next hurdle he had placed for his team – they were going to travel to Clyde Ohio in the middle of the season, to settle once and for all exactly who was the best football team in Ohio. Clyde High School, it seems, was in a snit over *American Boy* choosing Windham over them as the 1940 state champions, and Eberwine was ready to settle it on the field.

As Eberwine spoke, the ground under his feet trembled from bomb testing in the Arsenal. Some folks took that as an omen.

The Bombers returned an imposing lineup, with All-Americans Harold Stanley at halfback and Bob Turner at fullback. Joe Pinney was now settled in at quarterback, taking the snap and then flipping either to Stanley for an end run or to Turner for a pass. At the end slots were speedy Frank Janecek and tiny Bob Goss. At center was veteran Harold Belden, who had fallen in love with new classmate Mary Ammons, whose footloose father Duke Ammons, the author's grandfather, had moved the family from Fort Wayne Indiana to seek work as a telephone lineman in the Arsenal.

The second string backfield would have been starting on any other team in the county: Conrad Thrasher, Art Joy and Don Miller. The rookies on the team that year were Paul Turner, Tom Wedding, Dick Haynie, Glenn Ball, Melvin Brandenburg, and Ellis Maholland, freshly arrived from the coal fields of Pennsylvania.

In the first half of the first game that year, against the Shalersville Rams, every single one of those boys saw action. The Bombers scored 44 points in the first half, one short of the 45 point mercy rule, and just after halftime Bob Turner scored his third touchdown to make the final score 52-6 after just 21 minutes of action.

The Bombers were as strong as they ever had been, and everyone in the county knew it.

Mantua Township arrived the next week, and went home bruised and battered at the short end of a 38-0 score, in a game in which Joe Pinney demonstrated his mastery of the long-lost art of the drop kick, booting three extra points which counted for two points apiece.

Two games into the season, and the *Ravenna Record* was already predicting a Northern Division championship for the Bombers and salivating over a showdown with the likely Southern Division champions, the Charlestown Wildcats.

Except no one had consulted with the Hiram High School Huskies, one of the county's perennial sad sack teams. After all, Windham had dismissed them 40-12 the previous fall.

Both teams entered the third game of the season having given up just a single touchdown in two games. But the game opened on an ominous note, as the stout Hiram defense tackled Harold Stanley in the end zone for the first safety that Windham had ever given up. Then talented Keyton Clarke passed to end Stan Fields for one touchdown, ran in a lateral himself for another touchdown, and Harry Hurd added yet another. Windham's only score came on a triple lateral to Con Thrasher in the last two minutes, enabling the Bombers to avoid a shutout.

And so it was over. The longest winning streak in Ohio high school six-man football history, 21 games over three years, had been snapped – by a team that would lose to Ashtabula Edgewood 46-12 the next week in a non-conference game.

The game versus Clyde, which Eberwine had scheduled with such high hopes, was anti-climactic. The Bombers traveled to Sandusky County the next Saturday and fought hard against a team that was to go undefeated that season, falling 18-16.

A final game crushing of Mantua Village, 50-0, did nothing to remove the bitter taste of a season gone wrong. And to add insult to injury, the league championship game, Hiram versus Charlestown, was scheduled for Windham's own field. Hiram would win that game 28-26, with one of the most bizarre endings ever in sports. Charlestown's drop kicker prepared to boot the extra points which would tie the game – and misjudged his leg swing, hitting the ground behind the ball and breaking his foot.

And so the 1941 season ended, the final appearance on a field for the greatest collection of gridiron athletes Windham had ever seen. They had played together for four years and had lost only two games in the Portage County Conference. That same group of boys made the transition to the basketball team of Coach Dave Thomas and proceeded to claim Windham's first ever Portage County boys' hardwood championship with a 17 and 2 record – the beginning of a tradition that continues to this day.

But even as Windham celebrated its basketball victory over Streetsboro on December 6, 1941, Japanese war planes over Pearl Harbor prepared to change the lives of every single American. A two day wage strike against the Atlas Powder Company, under government contract to run the Arsenal, was abandoned that evening.

Food rationing was the first indication that things were going to be different. Housewives had to sign up for sugar distribution, and meat was to follow shortly. There were no bicycles under Christmas trees that year, because every single bicycle manufactured was appropriated for civil defense volunteers in each village in the country.

On August 15, 1942, the Ohio High School Athletic Association met to decide whether to eliminate high school sports for the duration of the war. The reasons were myriad: there was a shortage of coaches, as many had enlisted in the armed forces. Proposed blackout rules would have turned out the lights at night football games. The Department of War had ordered all buses to be ready at any time for emergency evacuations. And gasoline was now severely rationed. But six-man football survived simply by the nature of its small teams. Athletic boosters donated their gas rations, and a whole team could fit in two or three automobiles. And since six-man games were played immediately after school, the blackout rules did not affect them.

But even more than the hardships which the war occasioned, Windham was to undergo a transformation unlike that of any town in the United States. In the summer of 1942, the United States government bought up every square inch of available land in the village. It then contracted with the Hunkin-Conley Construction Company, a concern that came to prominence rebuilding San Francisco after the 1906 earthquake, and which in 1931 had built Municipal Stadium in Cleveland. They were to build 2000 housing units in the middle of Windham.

Almost immediately they fell behind due to material shortages. But the first workers of the Atlas Powder Company began to move into the new Maple Grove Housing Project that fall. The USO, that home away from home for soldiers and war personnel, began meeting in the Brick Chapel every Wednesday for the arsenal and construction workers.

New faces began to show up in the Windham schools in such numbers that Superintendent Deane Eberwine was overwhelmed with his responsibilities. Sadly, what he had to give up was coaching. The Portage County Board of Education, which then did the hiring for all county schools, assigned a young man not much out of college, former Kent State Golden Flash Kenneth Folger, to become the shop teacher at Windham High School, and Folger took over the reins of the most honored six-man football team in Ohio history – although he had never seen a six-man game in his life.

Although the 1942 season started later than ever before, Folger had little time to get acquainted with his team. The Bombers were lucky to even have a coach. The Edinburg Scots, Charlestown Rams, and the Mantua Township team, which didn't even have a nickname, had no coach and had to cancel their seasons, leaving only five teams in the Portage County Conference. Deane Eberwine, ex-coach and current Superintendent, volunteered to referee games, since there was a notable shortage of those officials, too.

Paul Turner, Art Joy and Frank Janecek were the only returning Bombers with any substantial playing experience, and Folger told the newspaper reporters he expected what he called a "redevelopment year." In others words, he didn't expect to win many games. An opening game loss to the Mantua Village Hilltoppers, 12-7, didn't look too bad, but then in the second game, against a Shalersville team organized only the week before and destined to fold before the season ended, the Bombers fell 10-6, and Folger's words appeared to be prophetic.

He shuffled his lineup from week to week, choosing from a cast of players including Harold Williams, Glenn Ball, Harold Rising, Harvey Warren, Richard Warren, Henry Dilley, Wyatt Carmen, Dick Haynie, Tom Wedding, Claude McManus, Ray Phillips, and Bob Horner.

Settling on a lineup of Rising and Janecek at end, Wedding at center, Ray Phillips at fullback, Joy at quarterback and Paul Turner at halfback, Folger, so well grounded in eleven-man football, finally began to grasp the fundamentals of the six-man game, and slowly but surely Windham began to regain its old gridiron flair.

Hiram came to town, and the Bombers avenged the stinging defeat of the previous year with a 26-7 pasting. The Deerfield Bisons fell in a 7-6 nailbiter. So the final league game of the season, against Garrettsville, would be for second place in the conference. This was the first time that Windham had ever faced the G-Men on a football field. The bitterest rivalry in all of Portage County began with a 19-0 shutout by the maturing Bombers.

All through the next spring and summer, the deprivations of a wartime society had become a fact of life. As fall approached, patriotic Americans harvested Victory Gardens, tool sheds were scavenged for scrap metal drives, and, since the 18 year old draft had been enacted the previous winter, many of Portage County's young men were in a military uniform instead of donning shoulder pads and leather helmets.

In Windham, a strange dichotomy had developed. The Ravenna newspaper always carefully separated references to Windham Village and the Maple Grove Housing Project, as if they were inhabited by different species. As a graphic example, on August 23, 1943, two boys were playing with pitchforks in the crowded housing project, and one, a nine year old, was speared through the eye and died on the way to the hospital. The newspaper reported that his family had "moved into the housing project *from* Windham less than a month earlier."

On September 16, 1943, Windham moved its first six grades into the new school constructed by the government in the heart of the housing project, a school which was later renamed the first Katherine Thomas Elementary School. At the same time, a new plaza was constructed adjacent to that school, anchored by a Marshall's Drug Store and an A&P grocery.

Football got off to a late start that year because so many students in rural Portage County had enlisted in an organization called the Crop Corps. Farmers whose regular workers had been claimed by the war effort could contact school principals for willing students to harvest potato, corn and apple crops. Until the harvest season was over, coaches had no idea from day to day who would be able to suit up for practice, as the players were often exhausted from a day in the fields.

Coach Ken Folger returned to his job fielding the smallest squad in Windham history, with only two seniors from the tiniest graduating class since 1922. Halfback Paul Turner and linemen Glenn Ball and Tom Wedding were his only lettermen. A bevy of boys, some from the housing project, dotted his roster, including new names Charles Spencer, Bill Ohl, Dick Pardee, Art Chaffee, Harry Hoskins, Joe Soltis, Dave Williams, and Ronald Smith, whom everybody knew by his nickname of Buffer.

Folger had one week to whip these rookies into a squad scheduled to face defending champion Mantua Village in their opening game. He settled on a lineup of Tom Wedding at center, Buffer Smith at quarterback, Paul Turner at halfback, Dick Pardee at fullback, and Glenn Ball and Harry Hoskins at end.

Coach Folger spent long nights that week mulling a game plan, and on the opening drive, he demonstrated the strangest play ever seen in six-man football. On a third down at the 40 yard line, the midpoint of the 80 yard field, quarterback Buffer Smith took the snap from center Tom Wedding, and flipped the ball to halfback Paul Turner, the younger brother of All-American passer Bob Turner. Turner spent the next ten seconds scrambling around in the backfield, eluding one tackler after another, until he finally turned and looked 45 yards downfield, where lumbering center Tom Wedding, whose yearbook ambition was to be a coal miner, had inched his way, unnoticed, along the sidelines all the way to the end zone. Even though most centers spent their entire careers squatting down with somebody's hands between their legs, on this one glorious night, that most ignoble of football creatures became the hero.

Wedding did not even have to move to catch Turner's spiral, a score that proved to be the ultimate difference in a 19-13 Windham victory.

Folger was to use this play, which the team nicknamed the sleeper, in almost every single game that year. Usually, it was Glenn Ball who sauntered the sidelines, appearing to flirt with the cheerleaders, before flying for the end zone to catch Turner's pass, often thrown almost the entire length of the field.

Oh yes, the Bombers were back.

A second game win over Shalersville 43-6 cemented that perception. Charles Spencer joined Turner as a scoring machine, as both tallied two touchdowns. The third game was trumpeted as a title game preview against undefeated Hiram, but it was no contest as Spencer again led the scoring in a 26-8 rout. Undermanned Deerfield proved no opposition in the next game, falling 31-0, with Windham subs playing the entire second half.

This set up the next game, against undefeated Garrettsville, as the championship game of the Portage County Conference. But there was one thing for which Coach Folger could not prepare.

The flu.

Ripping through his small squad with amazing efficiency, a tiny virus accomplished what no football team had done – it reduced the undermanned Bombers to a dazed, weakened shadow of itself. With only eight players able to even suit up, the starters had to play all 40 minutes. And Garrettsville, loaded with fresh substitutes, capitalized on it, administering the worst defeat in Windham six-man history, a thoroughly humiliating 42-0 thrashing on the miserable, rutted Garrettsville field which had been gouged out of a cow pasture.

A lesser team would have slunk off to lick its wounds, but not the Bombers. Having regained their health, every single starter scored a touchdown in their 42-12 victory over Mantua Township. They might finish second in the league again this year, yet they would finish the season with pride.

Although down to only nine players on the squad for the last game, the Bombers showed that they had overcome the humiliation of the Garrettsville defeat, whipping Charlestown, which had finally found a coach for their team. Paul Turner exploded for five touchdowns, becoming Windham's first county scoring champion since Ralph Drumheller had accomplished that feat in 1939.

1939 – Windham's first championship team, followed by the international championship of 1940. The Bombers had then spent the next three years watching other teams take home a championship trophy, and they were getting tired of it.

1944 brought very optimistic news from the European front. The Allied troops commanded by Generals Eisenhower and Patton had breached the Nazi defenses around Paris, and further east, American troops entered Germany proper for the first time in history. The United States had the jubilant feeling that the war would soon be over, and that our boys would be coming home. To further elevate war-weary homeland spirits, the War Department eased rationing on 17 items, including baby food and baked beans.

In Windham, the war continued to bring changes. The county Board of education transferred coach Ken Folger to Aurora, once more leaving the Bombers without a football coach. To the delight of Windham fans, legendary coach Deane Eberwine agreed to accept the mantle of Windham's skipper once again, and he had not forgotten a thing from his days as the creator of the most fearsome squad in the nation.

Although Paul Turner and Tom Wedding had now graduated, Eberwine had a slew of lettermen at the core of the team. His starters included Buffer Smith and Glenn Ball at end, county boxing champion Bill Ohl at halfback and Dick Pardee at fullback, newcomer Gordon Bertram at center, and at quarterback Freddie Campbell, a young man who had enlisted in the Army but was deferred, along with team captain Bill Ohl, until the day after the last game of the season.

There were only three substitutes available to Eberwine: Herbert Fechter, whose brother Robert had played on the 1940 championship team, Bill Alger, a skinny 125 pounder, and Robert Garrett Junior, whose father was a fixture on Windham baseball diamonds for years.

Opening with Mantua Village, Eberwine, who always wore a snappy suit as his coaching togs and a fedora to protect his balding head, unleashed a dazzling passing attack and a rugged defense in shutting out the Hilltoppers 30-0. The defense was led by Glenn Ball, who was so vicious on defense that he had the nickname "Musket," since his tackles sounded like a rifle shot.

However, in the second game, against Shalersville, Ball suffered a deeply gashed leg and had to be rushed to the hospital. Three of the four touchdowns were scored by second stringers in a 24-18 struggle. The next week meant a showdown with the Hiram Huskies, in what had developed into a nasty feud. Glenn Ball would be lost for most of the season, because the gaping wound in his leg had been sutured with a broken cleat still inside it, and the undetected cleat would not work its way out until the week before the last game.

But Eberwine would not be on the sidelines for that Hiram game. The County Board of Education had finally found a shop teacher to replace Kenneth Folger, and besides woodworking, he knew a thing or two about football.

35 year old Lewis Shumaker had played guard for Mount Union College in 1929 when they traveled to the University of Michigan and battled the Wolverines down to the wire in a 16-6 loss. For most of the 1940's, he had been superintendent at Thurston, a tiny village covering 3/10 of a square mile in downstate Fairfield County. Why he and his wife, also a teacher, came north to Windham is a mystery; all Eberwine knew was that one, Shumaker had never seen a six-man game in his life, but two, he was a warm, willing body.

One day after arriving at Windham High School, Lewis Shumaker's coaching debut was one for the ages. With Eberwine standing behind him on the sidelines, the Bombers destroyed Hiram 62-13. And those 62 points were all scored in three quarters, as the Huskies were spared further humiliation by the mercy rule. Sophomore Dick Pardee exploded for six touchdowns, and Eberwine could return to his Superintendent's chair, and teaching Pre-Flight class to budding aviators, with a smile on his face.

Then the season took a bizarre turn. The Deerfield Bisons, knowing full well that Eberwine had rebuilt the Windham juggernaut, took a vote and decided that a wise choice would be to disband the team and start preparing for basketball season. So Coach Shumaker, unwilling to rest his team while they were running at full throttle, asked Eberwine to schedule a game against the Bainbridge Bone Busters, a Geauga County powerhouse which also had an open week.

Showing that only one week's training was needed with such an abundance of talent, the new coach's Bombers went on a rampage, winning 66-13 in less than three quarters, establishing a Windham football scoring record that stands to this day. Buffer Smith had four touchdowns, Dick Pardee and Bill Ohl each had two, and Herbert Fechter chipped in one in the rout. But the Bainbridge team lived up to its nickname: Bill Ohl, Dick Pardee and Gordon Bertram all got cracked ribs, and quarterback Freddie Campbell came home with two teeth less than he left with.

But there was no one in Portage County who was going to stop the Bombers now.

Mantua Township went down 43-0. Against Nelson, Shumaker started rookies Bob Garrett and Art Chaffee, gave quarterback Bill Alger his only start ever, and even allowed ball boy John Hess to don a uniform and play in the 43-6 massacre. The only obstacle between Windham and its third league championship was Charlestown – undefeated Charlestown.

Was Shumaker overconfident? How could he be with so few boys on the team? He spent the week drilling the team harder than ever.

And with good reason. A cold November wind grounded the Bomber aerial attack, and the game devolved into a slugfest in the mud, the way football was meant to be played. At the end of the fourth quarter, it was the Bombers who clinched the championship trophy with a 13-6 victory. Those boys could well claim to stand equal to Eberwine's squads of 1939 and 1940. But junior Dick Pardee left for the Marines at the end of the season, so the 1945 team would be without one of the most bruising runners in the history of Portage County sports, although Pardee would eventually return to Windham, first as a player, and then as a shop teacher for several years in the mid-1950's.

The *Projector*, a mimeographed newspaper circulated in the housing project, announced in November 1944 that 590 units were to be dismantled. So even while the team mothers honored the players and cheerleaders with a home-cooked banquet on November 21st, and Coach Shumaker remarked that their clean sportsmanship was more priceless than winning the championship, there were notes of an uncertain future for the happy village.

May 7, 1945, dawned as a cool, drizzly day in Portage County, but not a single person cared that the weather was depressing. At 8 PM the previous evening, Edward R. Murrow had broken into the musical presentation on CBS radio to announce that Germany had signed a surrender agreement at General Eisenhower's headquarters at Rheims, France. One theater of the war was closed, but the battles in the Pacific raged on.

The Windham Bombers were well prepared to defend their league championship, but another type of bombers pre-empted their anticipation. On August 6, a month before football practice was to begin, and after six months of intensive firebombing of the Japanese mainland, President Harry S Truman ordered the innocently named Little Boy atomic bomb to be dropped on Hiroshima, landing directly on top of the city's largest hospital and killing 90% of Hiroshima's doctors. 140,000 Japanese civilians were instantly cremated. Three days later, the more ominously named Fat Man fell on Nagasaki, and six days later the most horrific war in world history was over.

The day after Japan surrendered, the Atlas Powder Company, the operating contractor for the ordnance center in the Ravenna Arsenal, began layoffs which, by the end of September, included its entire workforce of 5200 people. As a new day dawned for America, a post-war recession and population reorganization began in Windham. On that day, preparations began for civilian usage of the Maple Grove Project.

Columnist Loris Troyer wrote in the *Record-Courier* that Maple Grove had been a mistake from the start. The largest housing project in Ohio was to have accommodated 2000 families, but at its peak only 431 units had been occupied. Half of the 2000 units had never been built at all, the material having been shipped to a site in Michigan.

The *Projector* denied that the Maple Grove Project would be immediately closed and evacuated, noting that contracts for redecoration of 100 units had not been canceled. The Great Atlantic and Pacific grocery chain, however, closed its Windham store in anticipation of a great emigration. No one knew what was to happen in the village which had experienced the greatest population explosion in the entire United States during the decade of the 1940's.

Worries about the town's future drowned out the news that Coach Lewis Shumaker, after one year of glory, had resigned from Windham and moved on.

Windham now had its fourth coach in three years. And the man who took the reins would soon become a coaching legend in his own right.

Gordon MacDonald, the son of a Kent, Ohio minister, had recently returned to America after three years of active war duty, hoping to catch on as a science teacher somewhere near home. He had been a varsity tennis player at Ohio University. That he knew a little bit about football was good enough for new Superintendent R. Brown Jenkins to sign him on as head coach. That he had a lot to learn about six-man football soon became evident.

And he would not have the greatest six-man coach in Ohio history to help him. Deane Eberwine had resigned as principal and superintendent – resigned to leave Ohio, resigned to leave education, resigned to head to Florida, with which he had fallen in love. Eberwine was a Windham High School and Hiram College graduate, but had gone to the University of Florida for his freshman year, and he never got the Sunshine State out of his blood.

Uprooting his young family, he headed to the Tarpon Springs area, where he established a dredging company, became a real estate broker, taught scuba diving, and late in life became the public relations director for an underwater ballet troupe called the Weeki Wachee Mermaids. He left a football legacy that Gordon MacDonald would be hard pressed to fill.

The new coach had a wealth of players, so many that the county yearbook reported that they did not have enough uniforms and had to share, depending on who was in the game. Sending a defending league championship team onto the field for the first game in late September, MacDonald saw his boys fall 43-26 to Mantua Village. He had a veteran team, but he had not settled on any single style of play. His starters consisted of Art Chaffee and Buffer Smith at end, Gordon Bertram at center, Bob Garrett at fullback, and two newcomers, John Cain and a lad named Freddie Reichelderfer at the other back positions. Reichelderfer was a decent passer, but he was later to become more famous for the Freddieburgers he passed to his customers at the Brick Tavern in Garrettsville. MacDonald had a goodly number of substitutes to choose from: Dale Rarick, Harry Martie, Jerry Williams, Robert Blake, Ted Semplak, Robert Nathan, and a skinny rookie whose birth certificate said Raymond Myers, but whom everyone called Izzy.

For his second game, MacDonald relied almost exclusively on passes, and the Shalersville Rams had a field day with interceptions on their way to a 34-6 shellacking of the Bombers. In the third game against Hiram, he ordered Reichelderfer to throw more passes to center Gordon Bertram, who scored Windham's only touchdowns in a 34-14 nightmare.

This was becoming, truly, a season from hell. In desperation, the novice coach moved Bob Garrett from fullback to passing halfback. The Bomber faithful screamed in horror at this rookie move. Bob Garrett was left handed, and everybody knows that left handers make terrible passers!

But Bob Garrett Junior didn't know it.

The combination of Bob Garrett to Buffer Smith was the ingredient that MacDonald was looking for. In their first game together, Smith caught three touchdown passes and Garrett ran for one in a 26-6 win over Deerfield that at least stopped the bleeding. The next game, against Mantua Township, would tell whether MacDonald had turned things around.

50-0, with Bob Garrett scoring four touchdowns, showed that he had.

A close loss to a powerful Nelson squad the following week didn't change his mind. Garrett to Smith clicked for two more touchdowns in that game, and a final game win over Charlestown 32-16 at least ended the season on a high note. This victory was buried in the sports section as Edmund Peppard from Shalersville erupted for eight touchdowns to set an all-time league scoring record. On that same day, Mantua Village beat Nelson for the league championship – a Mantua Village team coached by Kenneth Folger, the man who had guided the Bombers for two years.

And Windham fans could not even drown their sorrows over the miserable season at the local bars. On November 6, 1945, Windham voters approved an election issue which outlawed all liquor sales in the entire township, except 3.2 beer.

1946 was to be a pivotal year in Windham, Ohio. The war was over, and Windham began to settle back into normalcy, but its origins as a quaint little New England-styled farming town would never return. 3000 people now lived in the Maple Grove Housing Project, with many more expected as the government instituted a Bed-For-Vets program. Married veterans from Hiram College and Kent State University lived, dormitory style, in Maple Grove. They rode the bus to school every day, and at night, well, the next generation is not known as the Baby Boomers for nothing. 452 newborns arrived at Robinson Memorial hospital in the first seven months of 1946.

The Ravenna Grotto staged the first ever football preview game at Ravenna Stadium in early September, alternating quarters between six-man and eleven-man teams. The purpose was to provide a medical fund for injured players. 5000 people showed up, the Grotto collected $3000 for its fund, and Windham, again led by Gordon MacDonald, the youngest coach in the league, topped Hiram 6-0 in its single quarter of play.

The Bombers had graduated only one senior, reliable Gordon Bertram, who left for four years in the Marines and a later career as a lawyer and judge in Monticello Kentucky. But senior Jack Flitcraft, whose family had moved into the Maple Grove Projects, fit right into Bertram's old center spot. And Dick Pardee was back from the Marines. Dick smoked like a Marine, cursed like a Marine, and liked to do his pre-game warmup in Clarkie's Bar, but he was still the best running back in Portage County.

The lineup that year featured Art Chaffee and Buffer Smith at ends, John Cain with Pardee in the backfield, Flitcraft at center, and slinging the football as only a lefty can, junior Bob Garrett, Gordon Bertram's future brother-in-law.

MacDonald had a huge group of backups from which to choose, many from the Housing Project: Jerry Williams, Bob Hess, Don Phillips, Neil Henderson, Harry Martie, Ray Harvey, John Irvine, Jack Minor, Van Simpson, Bill Miley, Ted Semplak, and veteran Izzy Myers.

He would need them, because the Palmyra Tigers and the Edinburg Scots had returned to football after years away, and the conference had adopted a nine game schedule. It would be a long season, a war of attrition on the battlefields of Portage County.

The *Record-Courier* took notice immediately of Windham's team. In the article about Windham's opening 38-12 win over league runner-up Nelson, the writer called this "the re-establishment of the Bomber dynasty." Scoring honors were spread among Garrett, Cain, Pardee and Smith, and it looked like Gordon MacDonald had a grasp of the Eberwine school of football at last.

Palmyra brought its inexperienced team to Windham the next week, and actually look a 6-0 lead into the second quarter. But touchdowns by five Bombers, including three by Garrett, soon brought the game to a merciful conclusion in the head coaching debut of a young man named Kenneth Jacobs, a name which Windham would hear many, many more times in the coming decades, as he was to eventually become the superintendent of the Windham Exempted Village Schools.

The third game was equally as impressive, a 32-6 win over Edinburg. MacDonald rotated almost every player through the lineup, and Dick Pardee rambled for three touchdowns, each of which started from outside the 30 yard line.

But the fourth game was against high-scoring defending champion Mantua Village, which had been steamrolling opponents by even higher scores than the Bombers. Their featured runner was John Hon, who was averaging five touchdowns a game. What a game it was – perhaps the most exciting game in Windham history. Tackling was so vicious that Hon sustained several fractured ribs, but refused to leave the game despite spitting blood and struggling to breathe. The score was 28-26 at the end of the third quarter – but the game had really hardly begun for the Bombers. Dick Pardee again saddled the team on his shoulders, and rushed for three touchdowns in the final ten minutes. The defense took the ball away from the Hilltoppers on every possession, and at the end the Bombers again stood on the top of the Portage County Conference looking down, victors in a 42-28 epic.

There was no letdown the following week, as Hiram was crushed 48-29. Mantua Village rebounded from their disheartening loss the previous week by scoring 73 points against Nelson. The talk of the league was Lindy Pennell of Shalersville, who was chasing John Hon in the scoring race after scoring seven touchdowns in one game.

But Windham wasn't worried. The boys swaggered through Monday and Tuesday practice as if they already had a championship cup in the trophy case. Coach MacDonald did not appreciate their attitude one bit. So on Wednesday, he installed a new lineup, yanking every single starter for a new group of untested youngsters, Harry Martie, Don Phillips, Bill Spencer, and Bob Soltis, along with Art Chaffee, returning from an extended illness during which Izzy Myers took his end spot.

MacDonald told his erstwhile starters that they would ride the pine until they decided that the team was more important than their egos.

And they sat there for the entire scoreless first quarter of the game against Deerfield, until one by one they apologized to the coach. MacDonald reinserted them in the second quarter, whereupon they exploded for 40 unanswered points. For the second half, he put his rookies back in, where they got valuable playing time, and his veterans got to see the game from the second-stringers' usual point of view on the sidelines. The Bombers won 51-0, and MacDonald never had a single problem with a player's attitude for the rest of the season.

That week, the town buzzed over three topics: the upcoming showdown with Shalersville and Lindy Pennell, the new American Legion Post which had been awarded to Windham, with officers Willis Sands and Ed and Stan Permowicz, and, more depressingly, the decision by the Erie Railroad to close the Windham depot despite a protest meeting attended by over 100 people.

Coach MacDonald stressed defense all week long, knowing that stopping Pennell was the key to the game. Pennell never got a whiff of the end zone all night long. Tied 7-7 at the half, the Bombers shut down every Shalersville drive, Buffer Smith and Izzy Myers pulled in long Bob Garrett passes, and the Bombers earned their seventh win, 27-7.

The scoring machine continued to hum in the next game, a 46-20 win over Mantua Township, and as the chill of November settled on the field beside the high school, and other schools began practice for basketball season, Windham had one final score to settle with the Charlestown Wildcats, their eternal nemesis.

One last time, the offense and defense both had to rise to the occasion. But there was one complication, one piece missing from the machine that MacDonald had built. Center Jack Flitcraft, who had started every game that year, was not going to be available.

Senior Van Simpson had moved into Windham at the beginning of the school year. He had not played football before coming to Windham, and was unlucky enough to tear the ligaments in his leg during the preseason. MacDonald, with no other alternative, laced a heavy leather brace on Simpson's knee and put him right in the center of the line. It was the only game Simpson ever started, but there he was, nearly immobile, anchoring the line for the championship game.

The game was deadlocked halfway through the third period, but sophomore Ray Myers, who had become a veteran during Art Chaffee's sickness, played the biggest game of his young career, snagging three touchdown passes as center Van Simpson was a rock protecting Bob Garrett from oncoming rushers. The Bombers scored four unanswered touchdowns en route to a 47-20 triumph.

For the fourth time in nine years, the Windham Bombers stood on top of the Portage County Conference. They had average almost 40 points per game, and Buffer Smith, Bob Garrett, and Dick Pardee were named first team All-Conference, with Izzy Myers gaining second team honors.

Even though Windham had gone through that season from hell only one year earlier, this 1946 championship team was so dominant that the *Record-Courier* said it feared that no Portage County team would ever defeat the Bombers again. Columnist Matt Fenn, in a mid-winter editorial, pointed out that Windham, with 107 high school students, and 700 students in its entire system, had a bigger enrollment than eleven-man schools Atwater, Aurora, Freedom, and Garrettsville. He jabbed that "Windham wants to remain the big frog in the little six-man football pond."

Apparently, this stinging rebuke was enough for second-year Superintendent R. Brown Jenkins to decide that Windham could finally bring back the style of football which it had abandoned ten years earlier. The Bombers were going to play eleven-man football.

So that bitter battle against Charlestown on the howling plains of November would be the last six-man game that Windham ever saw.

The Bombers would play a restricted eleven-man schedule in the fall of 1947, not competing for the league championship. Having graduated Jack Flitcraft, John Cain, county high jump champion Buffer Smith and rugged Dick Pardee, it was probably a good idea. And Art Chaffee was gone too, ultimately to become a Methodist missionary and school superintendent of the American School in Puebla, Mexico, until his retirement as Dr. Arthur Chaffee in 2007.

Izzy Myers was returning in 1947. So was Bob Garrett, who, with Myers as his catcher, had struck out 18 consecutive batters in an American Legion baseball game that summer.

In their opening game against Freedom, Garrett and Myers, along with running backs George Apthorpe and Jack Gill, made everything look easy in a 24-6 win. The second game, against Garrettsville, was even easier, with three interceptions and the Garrett to Myers passing combination producing an easy 40-6 win.

But what no one knew was that Freedom was to drop the eleven-man game in mid-season and revert to six-man because they only had ten players left on the team. And Garrettsville did not win a single game that season.

In other words, Windham got the patsies at the beginning, before the real teams showed up.

Their last three games were against the eventual tri-champions, the Atwater Spartans, Ravenna Township Bulldogs, and Suffield Big Red. Windham did not win another game that year. They would win only one game the next season. And then a new coach named Leo Kot arrived.

But that's a story for another chapter.

The Maple Grove Housing Project, although it was built as demountable, temporary buildings meant to be moved and reused after the war, passed into private hands after World War II. As late as the 1950 *Speedometer* yearbook, it was still being treated as a separate entity from Windham itself. It still remains at the heart of Windham Village, an ever-evolving part of town history.

The Windham Bombers played six-man football for nine years. Other Portage County teams would continue to play the sport until 1952. But there would never be another school that could claim to stand as tall as the 1939, 1940, 1944 and 1946 teams. They played on a level that is hard to imagine today, because few locals have ever had the privilege to see the sport at which they excelled.

And since a mere handful of those players are still with us, less than a dozen, we can't even thank them for wearing the black and gold with such talent and pride.

But they brought enormous local and national acclaim to those school colors, and for that, they remain immortal, remembered in these pages, and never to be forgotten.

The Leo Kot Saga, Part One

The 1940's were an incredible roller coaster ride in the town of Windham, Ohio. In 1940, the tiny rural village of 300 people produced enough incredible athletes to claim the national championship in the booming sport of six-man football. But at exactly the same time, worldwide events were conspiring to explode in Windham on a daily basis. The government took two-fifths of the township for the Ravenna Arsenal, land that would never again be lived on, farmed, or used to expand Windham's business base. Then every single inch of available land within the village was purchased to build the housing complex which would eventually become the Maple Grove Project. Because of Windham's vital role in the winning of World War II, and its subsequent convenient location for housing returning war heroes, 300 people became 3000 seemingly overnight, and Windham found itself as the third biggest town in all of Portage County.

Along the way, the Bombers had thoroughly dominated PCL six-man football, to the point that the Record-Courier editorialized that Windham should be ashamed that a school with such a big enrollment was still playing a small school game. So, in 1947, eleven-man football returned after a decade-long hiatus.

And the Bombers were terrible, just as they had been a decade earlier.

Coach Gordon MacDonald, the best six-man coach in the county, had great athletes in Bob Garrett, Ray Myers, Jack Gill, George Apthorpe and their teammates, but the other PCL teams had been playing eleven-man football all through the 1940's, and they had no intention of welcoming the Bombers by rolling over and playing dead. Windham won two games over patsy teams in 1947, and then proceeded to lose all but one game that season and the next.

MacDonald much preferred coaching basketball, where the Bombers were more than competitive. So, in the spring of 1949, he let Superintendent R. Brown Jenkins know that he had better find a new man for the gridiron job. Fortunately, a social studies position was added at the high school that same year. And a 25 year old Army veteran graduated from Kent State University.

And those three events brought Leo Kot to Windham.

Leon Stanley Kot was born on October 23, 1923, to Thomas and Stella Kot in Glen Robbins, Ohio. Glen Robbins was a company town of the Dorothy Coal Mine, where all of the men worked. Most died there, too. Leo and his four brothers, one of whom died very young in a tragic accident, grew up to the music of miners with black lung disease coughing up their lungs over morning cigarettes. Thomas Kot Senior was one of its victims.

I have been to Glen Robbins, Ohio. Rand McNally never heard of Glen Robbins, and a Garmin GPS couldn't find it. I drove to the Ohio River village of Yorkville, Ohio, the nearest real town, and asked how to get there. When I asked a municipal building clerk for directions, her eyes grew as wide as if I had asked her if she wanted to be clubbed over the head with an ax. Very slowly and quietly, as if this was a scene from *Texas Chainsaw Massacre*, she whispered, "You don't want to go there." When I explained that I was a historian and NEEDED to visit, she said, "It's winter- the road probably isn't open to Glen Robbins."

But willing to sacrifice my life for the history of Windham High School athletics, I inched my PT Cruiser across three miles of icy hairpin curves into a hollow in the hills that slope down to the Ohio River. Glen Robbins sits in a bowl between two hills, two dozen identical houses, many still occupied in one fashion or another. A community center advertised a Christmas event from three years earlier. The town straddles a hideous orange creek caustic with acid runoff from mines closed over a half-century ago.

This is where Leo Kot and his brothers learned to play baseball, basketball, and football, eventually going on to star for Yorkville High School, which played in a small school class B league against other river and coal towns – hardscrabble football without facemasks, a sport that molded Leo's character in ways that hundreds of his future players would understand.

In 1941, Leo's junior year, Coach Frank Lollini's Bulldogs featured Leo at fullback. They tied their first game against Bridgeport 6-6, with Leo scoring Yorkville's only TD. In the next game, against Barnesville, Leo had the only score in a 6-0 win. In the third game, against the Dillonvale Night Riders, named not for any Ku Klux Klan affiliation but because they were the first school in the area with lights, Leo intercepted a pass and ran it back for the only touchdown in a 6-3 victory. He was also the placekicker on the team. That string of sixes instead of sevens in those scores foreshadowed that Leo would struggle with the kicking game for the next 25 years.

Leo never played basketball at Yorkville, which was blessed with enough great players to win the 1942 Class B state championship, but he starred on the baseball team as the right fielder, a position he would play on various teams until he was almost 40 years old. In the spring of 1942, Yorkville won the Jefferson County championship, then beat Powhatan in the district tournament to advance to the state finals. A veritable monsoon resulted in the entire tournament being played in a single day. The Bulldogs beat Chardon and Webster in the morning and afternoon, but fell to Reading in the finals that evening, 12-5. Leo had one RBI in the loss, but what he gained was a sense of the grand stage of a state championship game. In 1961, he would pass that feeling on to a young bunch of talented Windham Bomber baseball players.

In Leo's senior football season, new coach Ted Sims moved him to the halfback slot, and Yorkville faced a schedule of nine games, eight of which were at rival stadiums. What Leo got this year was the experience of being a road warrior, of facing hostile crowds week after week, a situation he would have again in 1952 and 1953 at Windham High School. In his final game, Yorkville played Powhatan, which had a 25 game winning streak. Passing for one touchdown, running for another, and, finally, kicking an extra point, Leo Kot scored every single point in one of Jefferson County's greatest upsets.

Leo was nearly 20 years old when he graduated on May 26, 1943. He was NOT the valedictorian of his class. But he WAS a decent student, so why was he so old for a graduating senior?

Kot family lore holds that Leo took a year off from school to work for the Civilian Conservation Corps, a New Deal program originally established to deploy unemployed men in the development of America's natural resources and in forest conservation projects. Leo's son, Dr. Lenny Kot, who today is a federal District Conservationist in Colorado, tells tales of a naïve Leo riding a train to Oregon, flicking cigarettes out the window and starting a series of forest fires across the Pacific Northwest. There are also legends of Leo promoting fist fights in the camps, and making more money as a budding Don King than for his honest labor. But what he got from his time in the Rogue River region of Oregon was a lifelong appreciation for the lessons of the wilderness, which he passed along to his sons.

But the question remains – when did Leo go to Oregon? Congress cut off funds for the CCC in June of 1942. Leo must then have gone to Oregon no later than 1941, before his junior year in high school. So Leo Kot spent his last two years at Yorkville as a man among boys, having seen more of the world than his small river town classmates.

And when he graduated in May of 1943, he was to see much more – because the United States Army was at war with Adolf Hitler.

Leo's older brother Tom was already serving in the Navy, but Leo decided to enlist in the United States Army. After basic training, he was assigned to the United States Army Air Corps, the forerunner of the modern Air Force. His specific assignment was the 453rd Bombardment Group. Leo Kot was going to be a tail gunner.

The 453rd had been organized only two weeks before Leo's high school commencement. Leo was deployed to England with his group, where it was attached to the Eighth Air Force, and began bombing runs in B-24 Liberators from Old Buckenham Airfield in Attleborough. Between September 28, 1944 and March 21, 1945, Leo and his crew flew 35 missions over Europe. They bombed Berlin and Hamburg. They bombed German communications sites during the Battle of the Bulge. And Leo saw things that would haunt him the rest of his life, which he recorded in a diary of every bombing run he flew on, complete with terrifying accounts of flying through flak storms at 20,000 feet, and engine failures on over half the missions.

Coming back from a flight over Germany in early March of 1945, on his 30th mission, an 88 millimeter flak round tore through the rear of the plane, where Leo was seated, but did not explode. It ripped a three foot hole in the metal behind him, the heat of the entry causing some of his machine gun ammo to explode, and exited through the other side. If it had been fired one fraction of a second earlier, it would have blown him apart. The temperature inside the plane dropped to 40 degrees below zero. The plane arrived back in England safely, but Leo never took anything in life for granted again.

His comment that night in his diary reads, "Them jokers mean business!"

Leo saw many of his friends in the Air Corps die in crashes. The B-24s were often overloaded with fuel and ammo and sometimes couldn't clear trees at the end of runways, leaving nothing but a big hole in the ground. Once he left the service, Leo never willingly entered an airplane again.

When the war ended, and Staff Sergeant Leo Kot had received four bronze stars, he was as grateful as a human being could be. He was going home to a beautiful young woman named Mary Keadle, and home to play football once more.

The last word in his war diary, set off by itself at the end of a page, is "*Happy.*"

Leo's brother Tom was already playing football at the University of Nevada, but when Leo enrolled at Kent State University under the GI Bill, Tom decided to return to Ohio and play football with his brother. Kent State had suspended its football program in 1943, and the fall of 1946 would mark its return to the gridiron under its new coach, a brilliant but disagreeable man named Trevor Rees.

Rees was building a team around returning veterans, men who were older than most modern NFL rookies. And the Kot boys became the centerpiece of that first Golden Flash squad. This was the first brother combination at Kent State in decades, and the *Record-Courier* built a human interest story around this. Tom was the star of the spring practices, and he was installed at left halfback. Leo, larger and slower, was third in the depth chart at right half.

Both of the Kot boys scored a touchdown in the 40-0 victory over Hiram College to open the season. Tom wrenched his knee in that game, an injury that would hamper him for the rest of the season. In the second game against John Carroll, Leo again scored a touchdown in a 20-7 win. And then, in the fourth game, against Baldwin-Wallace, Leo broke his leg. Trevor Rees had no use for lame players. He told Leo that he was no longer on the team, a bitter lesson that Leo would remember for the rest of his life when he had to handle boys who had sacrificed their bodies for the Windham Bombers.

But Leo Kot was a fighter. Someone who had nearly been blown out of a B-24 was not intimidated by a petty tyrant like Trevor Rees. He gamely rehabilitated his leg for the next six months, showed up at spring practice, and re-earned his spot in the Kent State backfield.

The opening lineup for the 1947 Golden Flashes had both Kots in the backfield, and both of them passed for touchdowns in the victory over Mount Union College. Tom rushed for 40 yards and passed for 89, and Leo rushed for 24 and added a 10 yard touchdown pass.

It was the last time they would appear in a game together.

Rees had recruited many new players, including several who had graduated after the war and were younger and faster than the damaged Leo Kot, and his playing time began to dwindle. He made appearances in games against Miami University and Kalamazoo College, and then his name once more disappears from the Kent State roster.

Leo, now 24 years old, would never wear a football uniform again.

He had married Mary Keadle in June of 1947, and they settled into a barracks-type rooming house on North River Street in Kent behind Bissler's Funeral Home. He hit the books, came home to Mary at night, and looked forward to graduating in 1949 with a Bachelor of Science in Education.

Leo wanted to be a teacher, and even more than that, he wanted to be a coach.

And in the summer of 1949, as Leo and Mary Kot welcomed their first child Allen into the world and Leo needed a job, Windham High School, in a small town governed by Mayor Jim Purdy, needed someone to shape up their sad-sack football team.

Leo did not inherit much from Gordon MacDonald. The Bombers did not know HOW to win, despite having several talented players. He brought the T-formation with him from Kent State, and began teaching football from the ground up. The Portage County Conference had fractured into an 8 team league now called the Portage County League, because Aurora, Freedom, Mantua and Hiram had left to form a weak loop they called the Big Four.

Leo's first game against Atwater, a 19-0 loss, didn't even merit a game article, because much of the paper that day was dominated by news that Russia had exploded its first atomic bomb. That was the day the Cold War began.

That began a string of humiliating defeats by Ravenna Township, Randolph and Rootstown. What scoring Windham did manage in those lopsided games was done by Dick Campbell and Don Clark. The *Record-Courier* called the Bombers "improving", a word newspapers always use for teams that usually lose by more than 30 points.

For the fifth game, Suffield was coming to town, and Suffield was also winless. Perhaps it's fitting that the game ended in a 13-13 tie. But in the next game, against Garrettsville, Don Clark scored two touchdowns, perhaps inspired by the fact that it was Homecoming and both he and his girlfriend Joanne Chaffee were on the court. The Bombers exploded for 33 points; unfortunately, it was one less than the G-Men scored.

Such a scoring bonanza must have whetted Leo's appetite, because he hastily arranged a season-ending game against Boston Township, which the Bombers won 57-25, Leo's first victory as a head coach. Of course, this massacre is somewhat suspicious, in that Boston, a newcomer to the sport, played a game against the Rootstown JUNIOR varsity the following week.

Still, they had ended the season with a victory, which counted for something. And under Leo's picture in the 1950 yearbook, he earned a first-year teacher's highest tribute – Leo was called "a good guy."

In 1950, the entire student body sold magazine subscriptions to buy new uniforms for the team. They might not play very well, but by golly, the Bombers were going to LOOK good on the field. For three years the whipping boys of the league, opponents must have laughed at them prancing around in their fancy new duds.

They were stupid to do that.

Leo had installed the split-T formation to utilize the speed in his backfield. The newspaper called the Bombers "big and bruising" - they must have meant Claire Liddle, Don Sampson and Tom Nutter, who averaged 175 pounds, because they surely weren't referring to Pat Strohm, Don Clark, Al Kinney, Bill Cunningham or center Stan "Dodo" Permowicz, none of whom had ever seen 150 pounds, even in full uniform.

It took the boys awhile to adjust to Leo's new offense in that fall of 1950. They lost their first game to Mantua, which had given up only two points the entire preceding season, but scored 19 points in the loss. Another loss to Atwater yielded 13 points, and by this time Leo finally had the boys believing that they belonged on the same field as their PCL foes.

The wins started to come, first over Ravenna Township, and then a 40-7 win over Randolph under the lights at Mogadore, in a game that had to be halted by the police because disgruntled Tiger fans assaulted several Windham students. A one-point loss to Rootstown and a tie with Suffield were a momentary lull, as an historic 32-0 thrashing of Garrettsville and a final win over Boston Township concluded Windham's first winning season in their eleven-man football history.

But the joy in the small town was muted when news arrived that Bill Starkey had become Windham's first casualty of the Korean War. It would not be the last time that war would claim someone who had worn the black and gold on the football field.

Big changes came to Portage County before the 1951 season. Southeast High School was created from Palmyra, Edinburg, Charlestown, Deerfield and Paris. The James A. Garfield district was formed from a consolidation of Freedom, Nelson and Garrettsville. The Big Four Conference dissolved, bringing Mantua, carrying a three year winning streak, back into the PCL. And they would be the Bombers' first opponent.

For the first time, the *Record-Courier* mentioned the words "possible contender" next to the name Windham. Don Clark was the only skill position player who had graduated. At the annual Grotto preview game, Leo kept his starters under wraps, playing his second string so as not to tip his hand to scouts in the stands. The *Record-Courier* reported that the Bombers were outclassed by the Windham majorettes, who dressed in cowgirl outfits and managed to incorporate a live pony into their routine.

Leo introduced his starting backfield of Bill Cunningham, Al Kinney, Jack Christopher and John Campbell at the opening game against Mantua and their vaunted 27 game winning streak. The game article says that "the lighter and undermanned Mantua team was unable to withstand the assault of the heavier Bombers." Never was battle imagery better utilized than this description of a team guided by an old tail gunner. It was indeed a war on the field that afternoon, and a 13-0 Windham win meant that Leo Kot finally had his football machine clicking.

Atwater and Ravenna Township fell, and then unbeaten Randolph edged the Bombers 14-12. The losing became a streak with a 6-2 loss to Rootstown. Those were the only losses of the year, and Randolph and Rootstown ended up as league co-champs. Sadly, the joy of such a good season went out of the town when the Methodist Church burned to the ground on November 2, taking with it the beautiful organ which Andrew Carnegie had donated in 1915. But Pastor Warren Tropf vowed to begin rebuilding the very next day.

A season ending tie with Madison, in a game in which air temperatures were in the single digits and the lights flickered through the entire game, left the Bombers with a 5-2-1 record. Claire Liddle, Don Sampson, Jack Christopher, and Al Kinney made All-Conference.

In 1952, big changes were in store for Windham.

Jack Reay replaced Jim Purdy as Mayor of Windham. Mrs. Homer McDivitt led a temperance crusade against liquor in Windham – Clarkie's Bar was the only place that sold alcohol in Windham, and they were limited to 3.2% beer – and she succeeded in keeping Windham dry in the November election. Harbison Walker workers went on strike on July 30th, 1952, idling the steel mills that depended on their bricks for almost three weeks.

And Windham had a record of two wins and six losses in football.

What happened? Some of the stars had graduated, but many remained. Leo was certainly a more experienced coach. What one factor dropped a championship contender to the league basement?

The simple answer: the Bombers had no field on which to play.

Their field since 1941 had been a north-south configuration starting on High Street, today's Bauer Avenue, and ending in Charlie Curtis's cow pasture. But something else was now sitting on that land.

Today it's called the Marty Hill Gymnasium. And Ed Liddle Field, the modern football stadium, had yet to be built.

Playing every game on the road, with home games scheduled at Newton Falls or Garrettsville, had to be a trial for the boys. Their only easy game was against Southeast, fielding their first team ever. Junior tackle Stan Gill was the only Bomber to make the All-Conference team. And even worse, the new football field would not be ready in time for the 1953 season.

They would not have a single home game, and very few fans follow a loser on the road, which made what happened one of the real miracles of Windham athletic history.

The homeless 1953 Bombers of Leo Kot won the Portage County League championship.

Windham was basketball crazy by now. The 1951 and 1952 Bombers were Portage County League champions, playing in the 1928 gymnasium which baby boomers called the Old Gym. The 1952 team of Coach Clayton West was 25-1 and arguably the greatest basketball team in Windham history.

So no one much cared about a football team coming off a miserable season and with no home games even scheduled. Windham looked so bad in the Grotto preview game that the *Record-Courier* actually used the word "inept" to describe their performance.

Leo huddled with Dick Schlup, the newly appointed basketball coach and assistant football coach, and remade the entire team in the space of the single week before their opener, a non-conference game against defending league co-champion Ravenna Township. He moved team captain Norm Clark from end to tackle, Rich Bisbing from center to end, All-County tackle Stan Gill became the fullback, Ron DeCavitch, Curt Wirick, Lee Clark, Bert Spencer, and Ed Nutter were plugged into the line, and sophomore Lefty Bowers, who had to wear shoes at weigh-in to nudge the scales over 100 pounds, was installed at quarterback, sharing time with Bob Laymon.

Every day after school, the entire team trudged over to the pasture next to Maple Grove elementary school, today the outfield of the Bombers' baseball field, which was the only open space in the town big enough to practice on. But they had so much camaraderie that Leo was moved to tell the *Record-Courier* reporter, "I know Ravenna Township has the edge in experience, but the way our spirit and play has perked up in the last week, we just may come up with something."

They didn't. They lost 18-0, on a field that was no better than a muddy swamp.

One other thing needs to be noted. Leo Kot only had 15 boys on that 1953 team for that first game. But every one of them had the heart of a lion, and Leo knew that if he could only come up with the right combination, he could turn them into winners, so it was back to the drawing board.

Several more boys showed up, healed from injuries. Bob Laymon was moved permanently to halfback, Bill Donley joined him there, and Stan Gill made another transition out to end, where he was joined by Carl Ball. Steady guard Ed Ryan, who had been injured the week before, was replaced by Fred Parsons. Brothers Pete and Ron Rinaldi filled in the backfield positions. Ron Ash, Ken Rarick, John Lutz, Bob Lemon, and Bob Lusher were available to alternate into the line.

And of course, everybody also had to play defense, so there was never a break for anyone during the game.

The second game, against Garfield, showed promise. Bob Laymon scored both touchdowns in a 13-0 Bomber victory. Laymon, everybody agreed, was the fastest runner in the county, and had moves that left tacklers grasping at shadows. But his linemen knew a secret that opponents didn't. Bob Laymon hated pain, and he was scared of being tackled. He hated tackling drills in practice, and would do anything to dodge a tackler in a game. So the fans marveled at the boy's ability, though his teammates couldn't help but smirk.

The next game must have made Leo question his coaching ability, because Southeast beat Windham 20-13, the first ever win for the Pirates after two consecutive winless seasons. Almost 60 years later, Stan Gill and Norm Clark remembered the game like it was yesterday, because it may have been the most brutal game in Windham history.

Two Southeast players had been ejected for rough play early in the game, and later, a Southeast player kicked prostrate guard Ed Ryan in the head so hard that Ed fell unconscious and swallowed his tongue. A nurse raced from the stands and yanked his tongue back into place, but Ed, still unconscious, had to be taken to the hospital by ambulance.

Captain Stan Gill was so enraged by this that he punched the offender on the very next play. The Southeast player retaliated by punching Norm Clark, precipitating an on-field brawl which resulted in Gill and Ron Ash being ejected.

On the bus ride home, Coach Kot told Stan Gill, his returning All-Conference player and team captain, that he was through as a player, to turn in his equipment. Stan told Leo that he would see him at practice Monday. Whatever thoughts each had the rest of the weekend, Stan showed up Monday and Leo never said another word about the matter.

But what Stan Gill didn't know was where Leo had been that weekend. Ed Ryan lay unconscious in a bed at Robinson Memorial Hospital, and Leo had been by his bedside the entire time, repeating, "Ryan, this is Coach Kot. Get up." Attendant nurses later told Ed that every time Leo said this, Ed's blood pressure would spike, as if he was trying to respond to his coach's orders. And by the end of the weekend, Ed had finally regained consciousness, and Leo could finally go home, probably having forgotten what he had told Stan Gill.

Ed Ryan would never play football again. Despite his pleading, Leo would not allow him to suit up except for the team picture at the end of the season. When Ed, a very bright student, went off to Northeastern University in Boston, he tried out for the football team, but was called into the Athletic Director's office and told he could not play. The AD said Leo had called him and explained that the injury Ed had received at Southeast was such that any contact sport could result in permanent paralysis. Ed then realized that Leo had been trying to protect him without breaking a young athlete's heart.

Leo had learned a lesson from the cruelty Kent State coach Trevor Rees had shown him after his broken leg, and countless injured Bomber players would benefit from Leo's compassion, although they may not have realized it until many years later. And Ed Ryan later went on to serve four years in the Air Force because Leo Kot had protected his health.

After that Southeast loss, the Windham Bombers had a new mantra. It was *"Win it for Ryan."* Norm Clark and Stan Gill became the on-field cheerleaders for the tiny squad of boys who never had a home game and who all played nearly every minute of every game. When the team was down, the captains would scream that they had more to give, to play smart and play hard.

And they did.

The wins began to pile up. Mantua went down 32-6, with Bob Laymon scoring three touchdowns. The next two games were struggles, a 15-6 win over Randolph and a 12-7 win over undefeated Rootstown. Bob Laymon scored in each game, as did Bill Donley. They were squeakers, but they were wins.

On October 31, the Bombers beat 1952 co-champion Aurora 20-0 at Newton Falls, and thanks to a Suffield tie, Windham took over first place in the Portage County League. The final game of the season, against Atwater, would be the championship game.

The *Record-Courier* ran a huge three-column preview of the game at the top of their sports page that week featuring a picture of defensive tackle and team kicker Norm Clark, whom they labeled a "demon on defense." The game was at Atwater, it was their homecoming game, and the weather had turned brutal.

It didn't matter – the Bombers were going to win for Ed Ryan, and they did, 19-0. Stan Gill, restored to fullback and used mainly as a blocker, rushed for two touchdowns. Bob Laymon added one more touchdown to win the PCL scoring championship with 69 points. And Leo Kot, and Windham High School, had an eleven-man championship of their own.

Two weeks later, the team was honored with a steak dinner at Clarkie's Bar, given the more respectable name of Clark's Restaurant for the newspaper article about it. And Leo Kot was looking forward to defending the league title in 1954, on the Bombers' brand new football field. It wouldn't happen.

Instead, the Portage County League kicked Windham out.

It wasn't Windham's fault. New superintendent John Mensch, who had taken over when 51 year old R. Brown Jenkins passed away suddenly, saw the financial benefit in Windham becoming an exempted village school. The Portage County League was comprised of schools under the direct supervision of the County Board of Education, and since Windham had gone rogue, they were no longer welcome in the league. Thus began the Bombers' journey through four wilderness years as an athletic independent.

Although this was not a hardship for the basketball teams of Dick Schlup, who had increasingly brilliant teams which rivalled the best that Harry Kraft, Bob Jordan and Marty Hill would field in the future, cobbling together a schedule for a small independent football team was a nightmare for Athletic Director Leo Kot.

Leo Kot did much more than coach football. Every season since 1949, he reversed roles with his assistant coach and became the coach of the reserve basketball team, and then in the spring was the head coach of the baseball team. He was still playing competitive baseball in the summer, even playing on the county championship team, which had Duke Turner as manager, in the summer of 1958. He coached the Class E Hot Stove League team to county championships in 1953 and 1954. He originated the position of athletic director, which he then passed to Ed Permowicz.

Meanwhile, the Kot brood was growing. Leon Junior was born the year after Allen, and in fairly regular intervals a new Kot would show up, named Kevin and Mike and Billy. Mary Kot was the archetypal coach's wife, holding together the home life of six rambunctious men as best she could. A four season coach who also loved to hunt and fish with Bob Garrett, Ray Myers and Dick Schlup was seldom around the house. It was Mary Kot who made the meals at all hours when Leo returned from his unending scouting trips, and the hours spent analyzing game film with his assistants in the dark recesses of the high school. It was Mary Kot who was Leo's liaison with the Bomber Mothers. Leo could not have been the coach he was without Saint Mary by his side.

Beginning in 1954, familiar names began to drop off the Windham schedule, to be replaced by teams far removed from Portage County. Newbury, from Geauga County, entered the schedule to conclude the season. The Bombers had many letterman returning from the 1953 champions, but after two games, Leo had lost starters Ed Buck, Bill Donley, Ronnie Rinaldi, and Ron Ash. After failing to win in the first four games, the return of Bill Donley and his scoring prowess launched a four game winning streak to end the season on a high note.

In 1955, Windham's enrollment had reached 1000 students, making it larger than Ravenna City Schools, but 200 of those were first graders. The 1956 graduating class had only 27 seniors. Leo had negotiated with the Youngstown City Schools to purchase some obsolescent light poles and fixtures for the football field, but they wouldn't be installed until the last game of the season. Newbury remained on the schedule, but a new school, Crestwood, a consolidation of Mantua and Hiram, also appeared. Leo had only been able to find seven opponents willing to play Windham, every one of them a rugged team, since no coach unsure of his chances wanted to gamble on an independent.

Maybe they knew something. New names like Dale Kriz, Maurice Jackson, Tom Denvir, Wayne Hall, Bill Pelyak, Dave Rininger, Milford Hagans, and Larry Long had joined Lefty Bowers, now grown big enough to move to halfback, in the lineup. And when the Bombers knocked off defending PCL co-champ Randolph 21-6 in the opening game, everyone knew that Leo Kot had built another Frankenstein's monster.

In the second game, they beat the other PCL co-champ, Ravenna Township, 12-7, staging four goal line stands inside the 10 yard line to seal the win. A shutout of Atwater the next week kept the Bomber express rolling.

Preparations to face undefeated Crestwood the next week were briefly interrupted by the buzz over the bartender at Clarkie's U-Bar who shot three men who argued with him over the price of a shot of whiskey – yes, Windham had finally voted themselves a wet township!

Leo underplayed his boys' chances against Crestwood. The *Record-Courier* ran a strange picture of Leo's backfield gathered around him as Leo, kneeling, drew a play in the dirt. The only comment he would give the reporter was that "the boys are eager to go."

But they spun their wheels for two weeks, tying Crestwood 6-6, and then losing to undefeated Newbury 13-7 the next week. That would be the only game they lost that year. Garfield and Southeast both were thumped by several touchdowns, bringing the abbreviated season to a close. But the new lights had arrived, and Leo wanted to use them that season. So he did the unthinkable – he called Warren Harding High School, the Ohio Associated Press state champions of the previous year, and asked them to send their reserve team over on a Saturday night for the grand premiere. And he even arranged a preliminary game, inviting all his alumni players to return for a reunion game, with Duke Turner and former six-man star Bob Garrett Junior as the coaches.

The alumni game brought back a flood of memories. Then, as the Warren Harding Reserves took the field, it became apparent to the overflow crowd of 400 fans that Harding had sent most of its regular players too, outweighing the Bombers by at least 40 pounds per man, except for a very skinny, very small defensive back named Paul Warfield, who was elected to the Pro Football Hall of Fame a few years later.

Unexpectedly, playing the toughest opponent of the year, Windham won, 7-6, on a touchdown by fullback Dale Kriz. Leo Kot thought maybe that was his best team ever.

Until the next year.

The season preview for the 1956 team in the *Record-Courier* called Leo the "dean of Portage County coaches," a phrase that would be repeated every year for the next decade. Lefty Bowers and Don Miller were the only backfield men who had graduated, and the Bombers had added a kid at center named Bill Barker, who had moved in from Newton Falls. That kid would one day make Windham nationally famous. New names like Dave Flower, Ned Hertzog, Ron Wirick and Bob Franklin appeared in the preseason writeup.

New mayor Paul Lisec stole some of the preseason thunder by threatening to turn off the water supply to the Maple Grove housing project in the first of many tiffs with the Philnat Corporation, which ran the former temporary Arsenal workers' housing. At a council meeting, manager Bernie Cortes showed up with a container of orange water and bellowed, "Show me a glass of water that's fit to drink." Councilman Claude McManus shot back, "We could get the rust out of the water if Philnat would ever pay their bills." The water remained on, but the legal battles continued.

Leo had scheduled eight games, including pilgrimages to Newbury, Middlefield, and Goshen Union, over in Damascus in Mahoning County, and once the season began, he unleashed a scoring machine the likes of which Portage County had never seen. Game after game saw the Bombers winning by four or more touchdowns, marred only by a single 19-6 loss to Goshen Union, which ended the year undefeated. And in that game, star quarterback Bob Franklin was missing due to a virus, and untested sophomore Bill Isler received his baptism by fire. He threw two interceptions and did not complete a single pass. He would do much, much better in succeeding years.

After the Bombers season-ending win over Newton Falls, the *Record-Courier* proclaimed this the greatest team in Windham's storied history. But Leo Kot had only just begun to reach his stride. 1957 would be better.

Leo scheduled 9 games for that season, but before the end of the year both West Geauga and Randolph begged off, afraid to face this tiny team without a league. Ravenna Township, Southeast, Garfield and Atwater remained from the old PCL rivalries, but Leo was forced to go far afield to schedule Brewster High School, down in Stark County, and a new foe on the Portage-Summit line, Mogadore, with only one loss in the past four years, which would come to town for the second game of the season.

Most of the 1956 team returned, and new starters like Rich Gorby, Gary Mizner, Frank Gray, and Jerry Uldrich had only made the Bombers stronger. Ravenna Township was steamrolled in the first game, and then Mogadore loomed on the horizon.

Poor-mouthing Mogadore coach Ned Novell told the *Akron Beacon Journal* that Windham was at least a three touchdown favorite. He honestly anticipated no such thing. His team was four time Summit County champion, and he never in his entire career expected to lose a game, especially to a no-league gypsy team like Windham.

So when Bill Isler scored two touchdowns, Dave Flower scored one, and the staunch Bomber defense gave up a single score, Ned Novell was livid. He had seen his amazing streak, one of the longest in Ohio history, destroyed by a bunch of nobodies. The next chapter will discuss in much greater depth Ned Norvell's revenge, and how it altered the course of Windham athletics.

1957 ultimately turned out to be Leo Kot's only undefeated season, marred only by a final game scoreless tie on a bitter Saturday night against unbeaten Brewster. And Windham hadn't even practiced before that game; Superintendent John Mensch had closed the schools for the entire week during an influenza outbreak.

But one small event, outshone in coverage by Harley Miller's election as mayor, would change Windham's athletic history the next year.

Windham joined a league. There would be championships in its future.

The Tomahawk Conference, 1958-1961

In the late 1950's, a series of events occurred which changed the face of the modern world. Nikita Khrushchev became premier of Russia, Fidel Castro waged a guerrilla war to overthrow the government of Cuba, Elvis Presley entered the United States Army. And the Windham Bombers won a football championship that nobody remembers.

Over the next three years, Windham added 5 more league sports championships. This chapter will recall them from the shadows of the past, and along the way, reveal why Windham and Mogadore just can't seem to get along.

The story begins years earlier. The Windham six-man football teams of Coach Deane Eberwine, in the late 1930's and mid-1940's, compiled four Portage County Conference championships, and the 1939 and 1940 teams were even consensus state champions, but the eleven-man game returned in 1947 with the post-war explosion in Windham's population.

Young Leo Kot, the small town football coach who became the high school equivalent of Knute Rockne and Vince Lombardi, guided the 1953 Bombers to their first-ever PCL championship in eleven-man football, with a team worthy of a Hollywood movie. At one point in the season they were down to 15 boys on the team. They played every single game on the road, because the new high school football field would not be ready for another year. Led by quarterback Lefty Bowers, running backs Bob Laymon and Bill Donley, All-County tackle Stan Gill, who had been moved to fullback, linemen Ed Nutter and Curt Wirick, and linebacker Norm Clark, the lightly-regarded Bombers ended that season with a 6 and 2 record.

That same year, Windham became an exempted village school, a designation which benefited the school financially, but the net effect on athletics was that Windham found itself on the outside of the Portage County athletic wars looking in, playing an independent schedule in all sports. Traditional local rivalries were maintained, but a look at Windham's schedules in all sports in the mid-1950's turns up such unlikely matches as football games against Marlington, plus three schools which no longer even exist: Brewster, Boston Township and Goshen Union. The Bombers even played varsity games against the *junior varsity* teams from Alliance and Warren Harding.

Leo Kot had a special team in 1957. The preseason feature in the *Record-Courier* was headlined "Windham Grid Squad Short on Quality," perhaps the meanest thing a sportswriter could say about a team. But less than two months later, that same writer was forced to lead his final article of the year with "Windham aims for undefeated season". Kot had cobbled together a stout line featuring Wayne Hall, Bill Barker, Lee Oliver, Dick Gorby, and Frank Gray, with Gary Mizner and Bill Isler at end, to block for a fleet backfield made up of Quarterback Bob Franklin, fullback Bill Pelyak, and blazingly fast Maurice Jackson and Dave Flower.

Windham began that 1957 season with a 32-13 trouncing of Ravenna Township, and for their next game they would travel to Mogadore, which had already fostered a remarkable football heritage. Led by Ned Novell, their brilliant but arrogant head coach, Mogadore had seen a 30-game winning streak shattered by Brewster in 1956, and they were eager to begin a new victory run. Windham and Mogadore had seldom played in any sport, but the two small schools had signed a home-and-home contract for independent football games in 1957 and 1958.

So Windham's lightly-regarded Bombers played host to Mogadore on a mid-September Friday night, and sent them back home with a 20-6 defeat which must have set Ned Novell's teeth to grinding.

The next Friday, Windham defeated Garrettsville 39-13. By all appearances, a surprising gridiron juggernaut had been born. And then, on an otherwise normal fall day, all hell broke loose.

Leo Kot was a coach respected by every player who ever wore a black and gold uniform for him, whether it was in football, basketball, baseball, or golf. He loved to win, but he never wanted an opponent to leave the field of competition feeling humiliated. In those two lopsided victories over Ravenna Township and Garrettsville, Kot had inserted three freshman players, Buz Davis, Tom McCleary, and Frank Cassetto, who otherwise would never have received any playing time, because all three were destined to be cut from the active roster on September 27, 1957, and would basically become live tackling dummies for the rest of the season.

The reason for cutting them was simple. Every school in Ohio, on October 1, had to report their official enrollment to the state, in order to determine whether they would be classified as Class A or Class AA in sports, the only divisions which then existed. A school could declare themselves a four-year high school, in which case freshmen could play in any athletic event during the year, or a three-year high school, in which case only 10th through 12th graders would be counted, and freshmen would **not** be allowed on any varsity teams.

Every year, Windham declared itself a three-year high school. Like every three-year high school in the state, the coaches moved any freshmen off varsity teams before the October 1 enrollment reporting date, thus making sure that freshmen could not play football, basketball or baseball in a varsity game for the rest of the year. After all, the 9th grade had a basketball team, so the boys would get their playing time for that sport. In baseball, there were very active Hot Stove Leagues for the boys to play in. In football, however, they just became extra bodies at practice, soaking up experience along with their bruises, usually the butt of team initiations and practical jokes.

Besides, there were no football championships to play for anyway. Windham was independent, with no league affiliation, and state football champions were decided in the press rooms of the Associated Press and United Press International, with a state playoff system still 15 years in the future.

So Windham did what it did every year – declare itself a three-year school, send in its enrollment figures, and then receive a letter from the state, designating Windham as small school Class A. It was so standard that no one gave it a second thought.

Except Ned Novell, over in Mogadore, seething about the beating that Windham had administered to his team, which would indeed go on to win its 5th consecutive Summit County football championship that year.

Now, Leo Kot had NOT played freshmen against Mogadore, but Novell knew through the grapevine that they had played in the two other games before September 27. And he knew that Mogadore and Windham would, sooner or later, meet in the 1957-1958 Class A <u>BASKETBALL</u> tournament, and both schools had teams capable of advancing pretty far toward the state tournament. So he lashed together a plan that would both soothe his wounded pride and derail the vaunted Bomber basketball express.

Early in October, Novell fired off a letter to State Athletic Commissioner E. W. Emswiler, stating that since Windham had used freshmen players BEFORE October 1, they had no right to declare themselves a three-year school, that they had to turn in an enrollment total for a FOUR-year school and continue to play the freshmen.

That enrollment figure would make Windham a Class AA school for basketball season, and Novell could claim that the Mogadore football team had been beaten only by a bigger school.

And Mogadore would not have to meet Windham on the Class A basketball tournament trail.

The firestorm was immediate. This was a technicality that no one had ever broached before, over a common practice in hundreds of Ohio high schools. Novell also turned in Manchester High School for the same offense, apparently to cover his tracks lest someone accuse him of foul play directed at Windham alone.

The case was debated by the State Board of Athletic Control for a month. Sportswriters around the state weighed in. Larry Brown, then Ravenna Schools Superintendent and a former member of the Control Board, stated in the *Ravenna-Kent Record-Courier* that Windham clearly had justification for their interpretation of the rules.

Nevertheless, on November 2, 1957, by a vote of 4-2, the state board sided with Mogadore's contention, ruling that Windham would be classified as AA for the 1957 basketball season, placing them in the same division as huge Ohio powerhouses such as Barberton and Canton McKinley.

Bomber fans exploded. The Boosters Club demanded that the back half of the home-and-home football contract with Mogadore be canceled immediately. I remember Harold Belden, my father, one of the most mild-mannered people who ever walked the earth but a Bomber die-hard since his six-man football days, wanting to drive to Mogadore and thrash Ned Novell. I was only eight years old and had never heard of Mogadore, but I thought they must be drooling monsters to hurt my beloved Bombers.

But Leo Kot, basketball coach Dick Schlup, and Assistant Principal Andy Boyko saw salvation in another direction. They'd start their own league. One that gave out trophies, which Windham hadn't played for in five years as an independent.

And Mogadore wouldn't be invited to the party.

On October 15, 1957, after the Novell complaint but before the state ruling, coaches and administrators from five schools met at Southeast High School, all with a common purpose. The five schools were Crestwood, Southeast, Windham, Newton Falls, and Ravenna. All of them were Class AA (except Windham, for three more weeks, at least), and they all had grudges of some sort.

Crestwood and Southeast were relatively new consolidated schools created earlier in the 1950's. Crestwood was composed of Shalersville, Mantua Village and Mantua Township, and Southeast was a consolidation of Charlestown, Edinburg, Palmyra, Paris and Deerfield. They were substantially larger than the other schools in the Portage County League, and were generally treated like overgrown oafs resented by their smaller siblings. Ravenna had been an independent for several years, and was having increasing difficulty patching together a complete basketball schedule. Newton Falls was proximate to Southeast and Windham, and increasingly estranged from its Trumbull County peers.

And Windham was just mad. Spitting, raging, blindly mad.

The administrators who ran the meeting were Fred Swasey, superintendent of Southeast; George Converse, superintendent of Crestwood; Wayne Waters, principal of Ravenna; Andy Boyko, assistant principal of Windham; and Andy Pike, football coach of Newton Falls.

Pike listened to the talk and decided that Newton Falls had other choices and would opt out of further discussions. Ravenna did not want to play the others in football, but was in for all other sports. And Windham, Southeast and Crestwood were unanimous in their decision: a new league it would be, and they would name it at their next meeting, in November.

In the meantime, the decision on the Novell complaint came down. And thanks to that, one name immediately came to the fore.

The name of the new league would be the Tomahawk Conference, in honor of the hatchet job Ned Novell had done on Windham. Fred Swasey from Southeast would be the Commissioner. They would begin playing football and basketball in 1958, and track and baseball in 1959.

And they took an oath not to play Mogadore.

But there was still the 1957 basketball season to be played. As expected, Dick Schlup led his squad through a magnificent season. Buoyed by the same stalwarts who had conquered the gridiron, Gary Mizner, Wayne Hall, Bill Barker, Bob Franklin and Maurice Jackson, they rampaged through their regular season schedule with a 17-1 record, and entered the Class AA sectional at Kent State University's Memorial Gym as the fourth seed among big schools in the area. Southeast, their future conference foe, took them to overtime in the sectional opener, an ominous sign, and in the sectional finals against Springfield Township, stars Wayne Hall and Gary Mizner got into foul trouble early and spent most of the game on the bench. The lead changed hands 9 times, but by the end of the game the taller Spartan players had worn down Windham, and the Bombers lost 61-57, with most of their starters having fouled out.

It was a sad end to a glorious season – and it was the last game Windham, its enrollment boom waning, would ever play in a Class AA tournament.

But there was one more item of business to handle before the Tomahawk Conference could truly be born: the other half of the Mogadore home and home football contract. Despite the venom of the Windham Boosters Club, or maybe to relish his legal victory, Ned Novell wanted to play.

So on September 19th, 1958, Leo Kot took his Bombers and their 14 game undefeated streak to the unfriendly confines of Mogadore Stadium. Buz Davis, one of the infamous Windham freshmen who were at the center of the 1957 controversy, remembers Leo addressing the team before the game. Leo was a soft spoken coach, never cursing in front of his players except for an occasional "Hell's bells, boys," and his talk this night was no exception. "Men," Leo said, "something more than a final score is on the line tonight. It's prestige, men, prestige. We are playing for the honor of Portage County. Mogadore isn't one of us – they're half and half."

Most of the players, knowing little of county geography, didn't have a clue what Coach was talking about, that Mogadore straddles the Portage-Summit line, so perhaps Leo's talk did not have the desired effect. He was to do better in later years.

Windham lost 21-14, done in by interceptions and touchdowns called back by penalties. It was the last athletic competition against Mogadore for more than a decade. Good riddance, thought the Bombers – we have a new league to conquer.

A football conference with only three teams is like a bluegill swimming in a lake full of piranhas. Only two head to head games out of each season counted toward the title. But the rest of the schedule had to be filled – and that could only be done when the decimated Portage County League, from which Crestwood and Southeast had fled, had finished their scheduling. So the Tomahawk Conference did give these three teams a home, but it was still a hardscrabble existence that led to playing teams that were, literally, out of their league.

The 1958 Windham football season was nearly a carbon copy of the 1957 glories, despite the graduation of 13 lettermen. Maurice Jackson had graduated, but Dave Flower was back. Bill Isler moved to quarterback, replacing Bob Franklin, who moved to halfback. Bill Ryan, Bruce Ash, Larry Nutter, Gordon Berg, and Frank Cassetto anchored the line.

The inaugural Tomahawk athletic event was staged on October 2, 1958, with little fanfare. After the loss to Mogadore, Windham had rebounded with a 28-20 win over Ravenna Township, followed by a long road trip to Damascus for a 26-8 whipping of the now-vanished Goshen Union High School. And then came Southeast, their first Tomahawk foe, certain to give the Bombers a spirited battle.

The final score was 36-8, Windham.

The 1958 title game was on November 7, when Crestwood came to town. Dave Flower scored all three touchdowns in Windham's 18-6 win. For the first time in five years, Windham had earned a championship to place in its trophy case. And a legend had been born. Dave Flower, who led the squad in total yards, yards per carry, receiving yards, and points scored, was named to the All-State first team, the highest honor for a Windham player since Fred Stanley, Harold Stanley, and Bob Turner had all been named All-Americans on Windham's 1940 six-man International Championship team.

The inaugural 1958-1959 basketball season saw a new challenger emerge on the scene. Southeast High School had been consolidated in 1951, but had not seen success in a single sport during the decade. Coach Bob Ludick assembled a talented squad centered around Jerry Herron, Justin Martin, Dave Common, Chuck Wilson and Lee Owen. Despite the superb athletes from Windham's football team making the transition to the hardwood, Southeast won the 1959 Tomahawk Conference basketball title, claiming the first-ever trophy in school history to place in its showcase, where it still sits proudly today, although it has been exiled to a secondary display area in a remote part of the school.

Baseball seemed to get lost in the shuffle of spring sports. Game reports rarely made it into the newspaper, and yearbooks were usually published before the baseball season was concluded, so even won-loss totals are gone. But the record is clear: Windham won both the 1959 and 1960 Tomahawk Conference titles.

Track was always the odd bird for the Tomahawk Conference. All four teams competed, but Windham did not even have a track on which to practice. The conference meet was staged on the City Stadium track in Ravenna every single year, giving the Ravens a decided home advantage, so it was not surprising that they won the track championship annually, usually doubling or tripling the other teams' scores. Crestwood, in fact, did not score a single point in 14 events in 1959. In that meet, only Dave Flower, in the 220, and Rich Minter, in the mile, were able to break Ravenna's stranglehold on first place. Earl Belden took second in the 880, surely the only time the name Belden has ever been mentioned in any event involving speed.

When the 1959 football season rolled around, the schedule looked very different for Coach Kot and his Bombers. Goshen Union, Brewster, and Mogadore were gone, but consecutive road trips to Kent State High School, Boston Township, Marlington, and Southeast to end the season meant that the boys would be weary by the time the title game rolled around.

As the season progressed, Southeast showed that they were not the pushovers of the past. In fact, they had assured the first winning season in school history as the snow began to fly in mid-November. In the meantime, All-Stater Dave Flower had gone on to Kent State University, Bill Isler had moved on to Hiram College, and they were replaced by Dick Smith at quarterback and Buz Davis, Roger Tacy, and Tom McCleary at running back. Bill Ryan, Bruce Ash, Jon Rininger, Jim Burner, Chuck Apthorpe, Frank Cassetto, and Carl Valenti comprised one of the most solid Windham lines of all time. However, the tough schedule had left the Bombers with four wins, three losses and a tie as they headed to Palmyra for the title game. Both teams had walloped Crestwood, so that common foe was no indicator of who would triumph. Just to add incentive for the Pirates, it was their homecoming game.

Game day was cold and wet. Few fans even bothered to brave the elements to witness what would go down as one of the mightiest struggles Portage County had ever seen. Before the end of the first quarter, the field was a quagmire, and the nasty clay for which Southeast's field was universally hated coated every player, making it a nightmare for the statisticians.

After a scoreless first half, two third period scores set up Southeast for its first ever title. But Leo Kot was not called the dean of Portage County coaches for nothing. With the Pirates leading 14-0, Kot shifted the Bombers into a spread offense. The Windham drive alternated between Dick Smith bootlegging the slippery ball around the end while the Pirate defenders struggled to pull their feet from the mud, and Smith launching passes to ends Bill Ryan and Carl Valenti, completing nine of eleven passes in the fourth quarter under impossible conditions.

Smith scored Windham's first touchdown after a Southeast pass interference call, and ran the extra points over left end himself. After Southeast gambled and lost on a fourth and one at its own 45, Kot pulled the wildest card imaginable out of his hat. He sent Jack Steiner, the fastest player on the team, into the game. Steiner stood out like a beacon in his clean uniform, and Smith, after a fake reverse, found Steiner alone in the flat waiting for his screen pass. Jack managed to hang on to the saturated ball, and streaking as well as one can streak in quicksand, ran the ball 30 yards untouched.

One failed conversion for the Bombers, though, left the score at 14-14, and the Tomahawk Conference had its first, and ultimately only, co-champions in any sport.

The 1959-1960 basketball season turned out to be a struggle among equals (excepting Crestwood, which is the only school never to win a single Tomahawk Conference championship). Coach Arch McDonnell's Bomber squad was again led by football hero Dick Smith with his 15 point scoring average, and finished with a 12 and 8 record. Among those losses, however, were Ravenna and Southeast, so those two teams battled it out for the league crown, with a 50-49 overtime thriller going to Ravenna. The Ravens, coached by Clair Muscaro, who would later go on to be the Commissioner of the Ohio High School Athletic Association, were led by 6'1" Jim Cipriano, who was usually outsized by several inches, yet was the leading rebounder in the league that year.

If Ravenna expected to waltz away with the 1960 Tomahawk track title, Windham had a few surprises up their sleeves. In fact, the Bombers were leading the Ravens after the first 8 events, although the second day brought the inevitable result, with Southeast finishing third, and Crestwood at least being able to score this year.

Jack Steiner, whose last-minute catch had saved the Southeast football game, proved in this meet that he was one of the fastest runners that Portage County had ever seen. Running on a nasty, wet day on a soggy cinder track, Steiner clocked 10.5 seconds in the hundred yard dash, then turned around and won the 220 in the time of 24.2 seconds. Wrapping up his personal trifecta, he then took the long jump with a leap of nearly 20 feet. Only inches behind in the jump was Dave Schell, whose second place ribbon is the only Tomahawk artifact in the Windham Historical Society's possession.

Over among the weight men, Bill Ryan earned his spot in Windham history with a double victory in the discus and shot put. Ryan never really learned how to toss the shot properly, throwing it with a baseball motion that should have dislocated his elbow, but his immense strength enabled him to set a county record of 46 feet, 8 inches. Both Ryan and Steiner qualified for the state track meet that year, with Steiner taking fourth in the state in the long jump.

Although no one knew it at the time, as Jack Steiner was flying through the air in Columbus, the Tomahawk Conference, only two years old, was already on its last legs.

The Tomahawk Conference was the smallest league in the state of Ohio. Tiny, proud – but an undeniable freak. Forged in the fires of anger at Mogadore, it had in fact become a roadblock to an actual county-wide confederation, and the Portage County League wanted its prodigal sons, Windham, Southeast, and Crestwood, back.

Fred Swasey, the founding father of the Tomahawk Conference, was the first one to declare a truce with the PCL, calling for a meeting of the two leagues on May 19, 1960 at Ravenna Township High School. The meeting was chaired by Orson Ott of Garrettsville and Howard Cook of Aurora. Ravenna and Kent Roosevelt were not invited, since they would be too large for a combined league. Windham was invited to the meeting, but they refused to attend – refused, that is, until they were reassured that Mogadore had not been invited.

It took only two meetings for the union of the two leagues to be consummated. Coming in from the Portage County League were Garfield, Suffield, Aurora, Rootstown, Randolph, and Hiram. The Tomahawk Conference contributed Windham, Crestwood and Southeast. Streetsboro agreed to come in after its previous schedules were fulfilled. Atwater and Kent State High School flirted on the edges of commitment.

Competition was slated to begin in the fall of 1961, so the 1960-1961 school year would be the Tomahawk Conference's swan song – and what a melody it turned out to be, in ways no one could ever, ever anticipate.

The 1960 Bombers were as rugged a football squad as Leo Kot ever fielded. Center Jim Erbe anchored an impressive line, flanked by Fritz Everhart, Thom Griswold, Frank Cassetto and Roger Stanley. In the backfield, with Barry Hertzog stepping into the quarterback slot, Kot had a squadron of fullback Jim Burner, Tom McCleary, Buz Davis, Jack Steiner, Gary Wolfgang, and Rich Minter from which to choose. Out at the ends were Jim Moore and Jon Rininger, and the kicking game was handled by Paul Clark. From such a gathering of talent, you'd expect great things, and that is what the fans got.

Once more, Crestwood nosedived 36 to 12, and the championship came down to the game with Southeast in the middle of November. This was no Mud Bowl, though, and the Bombers came through with a 14-0 title game victory, finishing the season with a 5 and 2 record.

So the course of the Tomahawk history saw Windham emerge undefeated for the entire length of the conference's life, outscoring Southeast and Crestwood 146-46 in the six games they played.

The trophy they received for that 1960 championship is the only piece of Tomahawk hardware that sits in the Windham trophy case.

The 1961 basketball and track seasons brought no surprise at all, with Ravenna snapping up the final trophies in both sports. But the rivalries created within the tiny conference often rose to the surface. The first basketball game between Ravenna and Windham, a Saturday night contest on the Bombers' home court in December, was a ferocious affair. The Windham police actually had to restrain Ravens fans from attacking the officials during the 42-40 Bombers win. The bitter title chase between Ravenna and Windham continued through the entire season.
But in the last basketball game played in the Tomahawk Conference, Windham missed its chance to win a championship with an overtime loss to Southeast in the last game of the season, despite 18 points from Allen Nichols.

In track, Southeast climbed to second in the standings, with Windham third, and Crestwood, much of its team injured in a single automobile accident, again brought up the rear. Jim Moore took a first and second in the hurdle events, and it remained for Jim Burner, Gary Wolfgang, Charley Chase, and the Minter brothers, Larry and Rich, to pull in the rest of the points for the Bombers.

Thus ends the history of the Tomahawk Conference – except that it didn't end there. That sport I haven't said anything about, that sport that never got reported in newspapers and yearbooks, baseball – yes, baseball, would ultimately prove to be the lasting gem in the brief, shining life of the tiny Tomahawk Conference.

Windham had one of the finest Hot Stove League programs in Ohio, and coaches such as John Stamm, Dick Viebranz, Pinky Higgins, and so many others were funneling well-grounded players to the Windham varsity team of Leo Kot. All Leo had to do was polish them, and send them out to win Tomahawk championships in 1959 and 1960. But even Leo had no idea what would happen in the cold, raw spring of 1961.

The spring weather was so rotten in northern Ohio that when the state tournament trail began, Windham had only played four games, enough to win the Tomahawk crown for the third and final time, but hardly enough for the players to even get their batting strokes back.

Most of the boys had made the transition from basketball or football, although Rich and Larry Minter, Charley Chase and Barry Hertzog were doing double duty on both the baseball team and the track squad. In fact, there was only one member of the starting nine who did not play at least one other sport.

All he did, all he ever cared to do, was throw a baseball past, and sometimes at, terrified batters.

His name was Bobby Higgins. He looked 40 years old at the age of 17. He had come up through the Hot Stove Leagues, and he was good, so good that the Bombers rode him all the way to the state championship game.

At the sectional finals in Warren on May 12, Higgins, who had already won a game in the district tournament the previous week, was the starting pitcher against Suffield in the first game of a doubleheader. Giving up only four hits, he carried a shutout into the sixth inning, and helped his own cause in the fifth by singling and then being driven home by Allen Nichols' triple. A Jim Kline single scored Nichols, and Windham pulled out a 2-1 victory. Higgins had 12 strikeouts in that game.

Twenty minutes later, the Bombers took the field again. North Lima jumped out to a quick 2-0 lead against Jim Kline, and in the third inning Coach Kot decided it was time to go to Higgins again. Bob blanked the North Lima batters the rest of the way, striking out three, and Windham, propelled by a double by Barry Hertzog, managed to tie the game in the seventh and final inning. Al Nichols, who wore the thickest glasses ever seen on a baseball field, stood at the plate once more, and he clobbered a pitch to the far reaches of left field to bring in the winning run.

The Bombers had a week to wait before traveling to Canton for the regional tournament the next weekend. Once again, Higgins pitched the opening game, and twirled a magnificent three hitter against Middlefield Cardinal, fanning eight batters. As was their pattern, Windham squeaked out a 3-2 win on Chuck Schimmel's clutch single in the last inning.

In the second game against Powhatan, the Windham bats finally heated up in the cool weather, and Larry Nutter banged out three hits to go with two apiece by Larry Minter, Schimmel, Kline and Higgins himself. Jim Kline started the game on the mound, but when he loaded the bases in the third, Higgins trotted in from his left field position and took the ball from a worried Coach Kot. He got out of the jam, but in the fifth Powhatan roughed him up for three runs to take the lead, 5-4.

Kot brought Kline back in, and he managed to hold Powhatan scoreless for the next two innings. In the sixth, Kline smashed a triple to left field, scoring two runs, and came around to score himself, making the final score 7-5. The Bombers were heading to Columbus, the first Windham team in any sport to qualify for the state finals.

Kot was typically low-key in the week before the big trip. The *Record-Courier* couldn't get him to say much more than "the boys have been hitting well and we have been getting pretty good pitching."

Atwater coach Jack Cordier was a great deal more effusive. "That Higgins boy," he said, "is the best high school pitcher I have ever seen. His fastball, his control – he's almost impossible to handle."

The atmosphere was electric in Windham that week, but of all things, money was a problem. The Athletic Department had only $150 in their budget, not nearly enough money to put up the boys at a hotel during their stay, and that's when the true spirit of the small town came through. The Police Department, the Fire Department, and the Recreation Department all had shakedowns (better make that *fundraisers*) and Bud Mallett, Cy Smith, and Booster Club officers Frank Bushey and Gene Goodin gave enough checks to Athletic Director Ed Permowicz to cover all the expenses for the team.

The boys left after a pep rally on Thursday, May 25, and Superintendent Kenneth Jacobs declared Friday a school holiday. That morning, a caravan of 100 people rolled out of the village limits.

When Kot turned in his starting lineup for the game against Plains High School, which sported a 17 and 2 record, he had Higgins as the starting pitcher and Larry Minter as his catcher. The infield showed Chuck Schimmel at first, Barry Hertzog at second, Larry Nutter at shortstop, and team captain John Freudiger, whose .300 batting average was actually the lowest on the team, at third. Patrolling the outfield would be Jim Kline, Al Nichols, and Olan Booher.

A sunny day that May would have been rare indeed, so a 45 minute rain delay to open the game was pretty much par for the course. Didn't make much difference – Windham had come to play. Scoring almost at will, run after run crossed the plate, and Higgins worked the first five innings, striking out seven, but walking seven also. Kot probably should have brought his reliever in sooner, because of the long wait during Bomber at bats and the total pitch count, but he wanted to make sure the game was well out of reach before he called Kline from the bullpen. Plains went down 14-2, Windham had advanced to the title game less than 24 hours away... and Bobby Higgins had a tired arm.

Liberty Benton, the defending state champion, would be the final game opponent for the Bombers. Liberty Benton had won 29 straight games, had destroyed undefeated Coldwater in their semi-final match, and Windham was playing just their eleventh game of the year - for the championship of the state of Ohio.

There was one person on the team who had been to a state championship game before, and that was Coach Leo Kot himself. He wasn't fazed by playing a defending state champion, and he refused to let his boys be intimidated, either. He made only one lineup change, substituting Charley Chase for Olan Booher, who had sprained his ankle in the semi-final. Bob Higgins took the mound – Bob Higgins, who had already won or relieved in every single tournament game – and Bob Higgins rose to the occasion.

Inning after inning he shut down the Liberty Benton batters. Not a single runner crossed the plate, despite several hits and increasing Higgins wildness. Windham pushed across a run in the third when Barry Hertzog almost took the catcher's head off in a collision, forcing him to drop the ball. Another Windham run came in a later inning without a single base hit. Liberty pitcher Jim Reed held the Bombers to three hits, striking out 13, yet was losing 2-0, with one single at-bat to go in the seventh inning.

Higgins had trouble finding the plate, and walked the first two batters in the seventh. The next Liberty batter attempted to bunt with both runners moving, but missed. Catcher Larry Minter fired to third, but John Freudiger had been been charging the bunt and there was no one covering the base. The ball sailed into the outfield and Liberty Benton had their first run. With nobody out, the runner on second was then sacrificed to third, scoring on a slow infield out. The game was now tied 2-2. Higgins had not given up a hit, but the game now went to extra innings.

Windham did not score in the eighth and ninth inning. Bob Higgins, Windham's Iron Horse, remained on the mound. By now, Higgins had nothing left in his arm, and was truly pitching more with his gigantic heart. In the bottom of the ninth, with two on and two out, Jim Johnson clubbed a long fly ball headed straight for the outfield wall. Centerfielder Allen Nichols, whose batting skill had carried the Bombers to this point in the season, set sail for left center, sprinting, reaching out – and the ball hit his glove and bounced away.

Inches, mere inches – that's how close Windham came to the only state tournament championship in its history. So close – but it was the runner-up trophy that came back with them, and now sits in the high school trophy case.

And that was it. Windham did not make it back to a championship game until the magical 2002 baseball season, 41 years later. Bobby Higgins, his arm worn out by his heroic effort, never achieved his dream of a professional career, and like so many Windham sports legends, died much, much too young.

May 27, 1961, was the last day in the existence of the Tomahawk Conference. On May 28, 1961, the memory of this remarkable little league began to fade.

The reunited Portage County League had a wonderful run, from 1961 to 2005. It was replaced in that year by the Portage Trail Conference. Someday that too will disappear, to reconfigure and reappear as something new. Windham endures, but leagues don't. It's the nature of things. The Tomahawk Conference couldn't last forever. It was fun, and then it was gone, leaving only one trace.

Bomber fans <u>still</u> haven't forgiven Ned Novell, and although their rivalries were restored many years later, there has never been any love lost between the athletes of Windham and the athletes of Mogadore.

The Leo Kot Saga, Part Two

By 1958, Leo Kot had added a new duty to his Social Studies and occasional health and gym classes. Andrew Boyko had been promoted to principal, and someone had to take over his job as driver training instructor. That would be Leo.

In the 1957 *Twin Pines* Yearbook is a badly-posed picture of Leo and Superintendent John Mensch looking over the new textbook for Driver Training, with the athletic name of "Sportsmanlike Driving."

Hundreds and hundreds of Windham High School students, and some community members who had never received a license, were taught to drive by Leo Kot, many during the summer, as I was, with Leo in the passenger seat, a student (or sometimes an elderly woman like my mother) driving, and three terrified teenagers sitting in the back seat with visions of twisted steel dancing in their minds. But Leo never seemed perturbed by the thousands of times he revisited this scenario, usually on a trip to the Hot Dog Shoppe in Warren.

Every one of his former students has their own Leo Kot driver training story. My future wife Helena got substantially more car time than anyone else, because Leo would always pick her up first and drop her off last every day. Not that she needed the extra time – well, actually, she did – but Leo knew that her mother Ida Kukuljevic would always have breakfast ready for him when he arrived, and lunch when they returned.

A well-fed Leo was a sleepy Leo, and a probably-true story is still extant of Leo telling an early morning student to keep driving until he told him to stop, and then proceed to fall asleep as the obedient student drove almost all the way to Pittsburgh.

So Leo was a utilitarian teacher. He wasn't the best one Windham had, but he was far from the worst. If some of his teaching seemed distracted at time, it was undoubtedly because he was the hardest working man in the Windham School system.

Creating new leagues was not in his job description, but that was what fell to him in the fall of 1957, after the crushing defeat of Mogadore and its unexpected fallout. Leo, Andy Boyko and Dick Schlup were the guiding lights in the creation of the Tomahawk Conference, an affiliation of four nomadic teams, Crestwood, Southeast, Ravenna, and Windham, whom nobody wanted in their league.

New faces appeared on Leo's staff during the Tomahawk years. Dick Schlup had moved on to a position as basketball coach at the Ashtabula branch of Kent State University in preparation for a career in college administration, and his basketball replacement was Arch McDonnell, who became Leo's football assistant. For the first time, a third coach joined the staff, the new track coach, Joe Konstantinos.

During the three years of the Tomahawk Conference, Leo guided the careers of All-State first team halfback Dave Flower, future athletic directors Bill Isler and Jim Burner, Windham Hall of Famers Bill Ryan and Maurice Jackson, future mayor Jim Moore, All-State track star Jack Steiner, the baseball career of the phenomenal Bobby Higgins, and many more players who got to carry Leo's influence for the rest of their lives.

When the Tomahawk Conference dissolved in early 1961, after Leo had taken his Bombers baseball team all the way to the state championship game, Windham re-entered a humbled Portage County League which no longer held its nose at the idea of playing an exempted village school. The fall of 1961 was not a good year for the Bombers to step up in competition. They would be playing teams they had never seen before, both inside the league and out, since Leo added an opening game against the Reserve team from Alliance High School. And the graduation class of 1961 had contained some of the greatest athletes in Windham history.

So it's no surprise that more people, including Mayor Robert Nuttall, were excited by Windham's late August Sesqui-Centennial, which 25,000 people attended, than the Bombers football team. Although Leo valiantly told the *Record-Courier* that "we may surprise somebody, although this is the smallest team we've had in a long time," the reporter also got him to admit that "we have lots of lettermen around, because we give letters to everyone when we win a championship."

Something new was in the air, however. Cy Smith, a Windham basketball star from the 1930's, had started a PeeWee football team. Little kids running around in football gear was a novelty everybody enjoyed, and names like Allen Kot, Larry Steiner, Jerry Downey, Dave Qualls, and Ozzie Pinson began appearing in tiny print in the back of the sports pages. One day far in the future, they would move to the headlines.

Despite the heroics of great running backs like Darryl King, Charlie Chase and end Chuck Schimmel, the Bombers suffered through their most miserable season since 1952, flopping to a 2 and 7 record. In the Newton Falls game alone, Tom Turner broke his foot, Dean Gaskell dislocated his knee, Terry Purdy broke his arm, and Darryl King separated his shoulder. It was that kind of season.

It didn't get any better in 1962. Long time athletic booster Duke Turner was now the Mayor of Windham, the Windham Rockets won the State Class F Hot Stove Title, new basketball coach Bob Jordan arrived from Holgate High School to take over the reigns from Tomahawk era mentor Harry Kraft, who went into private business – and the Windham Bombers football team remained as hapless as the year before.

Leo knew what the year would be like. Along with his assistants, shop teacher Oscar Tentler and gruff John Lowry, who had served in both the Navy AND the Marines before going into teaching, he knew he didn't have the horses to keep up in the PCL race. It was worse than he could have imagined. The real star of the team was Joe Fabry, probably the greatest, and certainly the hardest working, punter in Windham history. The Bombers were shut out in four games, even with workhorses like Darryl King and Dale Stocker, and linemen like Jerome McDaniel and Joe Lutz, who managed to get tossed out of all but two games. They scored only eight touchdowns all season. But three of those touchdowns were tallied by a freshman named Ray Ruff, a name that Portage County would learn well in the coming years.

Windham made the national news in the fall of 1963 when it elected the youngest mayor in Ohio, 1958 WHS graduate Bill Barker, who had starred on both the gridiron and the basketball court. On the football field, 1963 started out like the movie *Groundhog Day* - a 6-0 squeaker win over Newton Falls to start the season, followed by three consecutive losses, two by shutout, although one of those was to Randolph, which would claim the mythical state football title that year. But Leo was cementing a rock-solid line featuring Phil Snyder, Bob Weeks, Terry Purdy, John Grafton, and Alan Jacobs, with Jerry Miller and vicious blocker Bruce Rininger at end. All he needed to do now was get his running backs in order.

Ray Ruff at halfback and Olan Booher at quarterback were the givens. Jim Honobach and Jim Mansfield were the other starters, but a bevy of sophomores gained a lot of playing time in every game. In fact, in the first four games, Leo had played nearly every boy on the team in every game.

Then, halfway through the season, things turned around. The Bombers started jelling, the points started coming, and Streetsboro, Rootstown, and Garrettsville fell in quick succession. Only a late season loss to Southeast marred the comeback. The final mark was 4-4, but the groundwork had been laid. Before the last game of the season, Leo made perhaps the most brash statement he had ever given a reporter, saying that the Bombers had gotten "tired of being pushed around, and just did something about it." Bob Weeks represented the rugged Windham linemen on the All-Conference team, and Leo Kot had given the PCL a warning for 1964, if they were paying attention.

Leo Kot now had a fabulous quarterback named Roger Stier, probably second only to Bobby Higgins in the lore of great Windham arms. Ray Ruff, still only a junior, was widely acclaimed as the best running back in the league. Bruce Rininger had been shifted to fullback to clear a path for Ruff, and there was no linebacker in the league that Rininger couldn't destroy. The ends were solid with captain Jerry Miller and converted halfback Larry Barker, but John Grafton was the only starter returning in the interior line. So Kot had to use a rotating lineup of underclassmen, and in the season preview, he said that "we have the boys to do the job."

Losses to Newton Falls and Aurora, the eventual league champion, to open the season demonstrated that the line needed to grow up quickly. Moving senior John Grafton to guard, he paired him with a floating rotation of sophomore Tim Stamm and junior Arnie Kesling, shifted center Bill Ingraham to tackle, and decided to take a chance at the other tackle spot on a chubby sophomore who had been too heavy to play PeeWee football, and had instead been Bruce Rininger's personal tackling dummy since the age of twelve, playing as a seventh grader on the freshman team. His name was George Belden.

A first victory over Crestwood cinched that inexperienced lineup, with last year's state champion, Randolph, up next on the Tigers field. It was one of the most bruising games Portage County had ever seen, an epic battle in the trenches. On the last play of the game, with the game tied 6-6, Kot pulled a new trick out of his coaching bag. He had often toyed with the latest innovations he had picked up at coaching clinics and from the innumerable coaching books in his library, but he only did it in practice. Leo had always told his assistants that "if you need to defend against something, you need to understand it first." In games, he usually fell back on his tried and true formations.

Not now. With the Bombers on their own 35, Leo had his backfield shift into the radical new formation today widely known as the shotgun, with rifle armed Roger Stier as the trigger. While the rookie linemen held off the onrushing Tigers, Stier calmly pitched the ball 40 yards downfield to a flying Ray Ruff, who outleaped four Randolph defenders, wrestled the ball loose, and sprinted the final 25 yards for a Bomber victory.

Except for one thing. There was a yellow flag lying on the ground where Ruff had made his catch. Ruff had not committed a violation; in fact, there was no penalty. But the official on the spot had ruled the play a simultaneous catch between Ruff and a defensive back. A simultaneous catch goes to the offensive team, but the ball is dead at that spot and cannot be advanced. Game over.

The Bombers went on to romp over their last four foes, outscoring them 104-20. Ray Ruff scored at least two touchdowns in each game. So it was no surprise when Ruff, Rininger, and junior linebacker Arnie Kesling made first team All-Conference after the Bombers' second place PCL finish.

During the subsequent baseball season, Leo had to save the life of that great quarterback, Roger Stier. Stier accidentally stuck his hand through a study hall window, cutting his wrist down to the bone, and only Leo's quick thinking and tourniquet skills stopped the spurting blood. After Dr. Nathan Chang sewed Stier up, Leo reminded him that he was pitching for the league championship that Friday. Leo expected a Bomber to be tough.

The 1965 Bombers had virtually the entire line returning, but the backfield underwent another redesign. Allen Kot, the coach's firstborn, moved into the quarterback slot. Larry Barker shifted to end, teaming with junior Bill Hall. Pete Bennett replaced the graduated Rininger at fullback. And now there were two Ruff brothers in the backfield.

Ray was shorter and more muscular than his brother Danny, who was more agile and as fast as a cheetah. Ray punished tacklers, and Danny made them miss, the most elusive runner Leo had coached since Bob Laymon on the immortal 1953 PCL champions. Kot thought that this was his dream team; for the first time ever, he called his Bombers "contenders" in the *Record-Courier* preseason tabloid.

A season opening loss to Newton Falls didn't change his opinion. He had molded the team for the PCL race, and his boys responded. Game after league game came and went with wins for the Bombers, five in a row, with the Ruff brothers decimating opponents just like the Kot boys had done at Yorkville and Kent State. It must have felt like déjà vu to Leo.

But the season was headed for a showdown, because the penultimate game would be versus Aurora, which carried a two year undefeated streak through the season, and the Greenmen had future College Hall of Famer Tom Curtis at quarterback. It promised everything a fan could ever hope to see – an All-State quarterback on one team, and the two fastest running backs in Ohio on the other.

Played in Aurora on a Saturday afternoon, on a rock-strewn field with Route 82 only a few yards behind the end zone, the Greenmen came onto the field with the words "Beat Windham" tattooed with electrician's tape on every helmet. Aurora held Windham to minus yardage in the first quarter, and Curtis hit halfback Jeff Jewett with a 10 yard scoring pass in the second. The Bombers immediately retaliated with a drive culminating with Allen Kot bootlegging the ball for the final yards.

The rest of the game was deadlocked, with the Bombers battering the Greenies but being turned away from the end zone twice. Ray Ruff sprinted 41 yards on a breakaway, but lost the ball on the one yard line to a vicious tackle. The Bombers drove the field in the last minute of play, but Curtis, who had been outplayed by Allen Kot, intercepted the last pass in the end zone to end the game.

It was a game for the ages, which made it almost criminal that Windham lost. Aurora had made their extra points, and the Bombers hadn't.

A final win against Garrettsville couldn't remove the bitter taste of a second consecutive bridesmaid spot in the PCL. Leo Kot didn't know if he could go through it one more time. He would lose Ray Ruff, Larry Barker, Arnie Kesling, Pete Bennett, plus reliable linemen like Don Henley, Eddie Qualls, Harry Purdy, Joe DeCavitch and more, and he wasn't sure that what was left would be good enough.

Windham was changing in 1966. Willis Sands had served a short stint as mayor, to be replaced by the ubiquitous Cy Smith. And Leo Kot was changing. Over the last couple seasons, he had seemed unusually tired. He retired from coaching basketball because of it. Windham dropped the baseball team that spring, relieving him of another duty, although he took on the job of head golf coach, which was at least more relaxing, since the coaches played each other while their teams competed.

Leo was coming to rely more on his assistants, whom he had molded in his image. Jim Burner was one of his own, graduating in 1961, playing four years at St. Olaf College in Minnesota, and then coming home to teach. John Lowry, the terrifying ex-Marine whom many thought played bad cop to Leo's good cop, had been toned down, and some might even say civilized, by Leo's understanding of the psychology it took to get eleven teenagers to work together as a team. Because whatever else they might have been, these WERE teenagers, volunteering to break their bodies in a black and gold uniform.

Leo worked as hard as ever. He was obsessively organized, like his idol, Woody Hayes. He instinctively knew what would work with any combination of athletes, and that's how he pulled together his practice plans. His assistants hated his conferences, always held in the tiny coaches' cubicle in the corner of the locker room, the air blue with the smoke from Leo's omnipresent Chesterfield cigarettes, Leo sitting on the toilet wearing only an athletic supporter, a sight his players just took for granted. But as the 1966 season approached, Leo had thoughts which he shared with absolutely none of his staff or players.

But the first order of business was to remold his line. He had three year starters George Belden and Tim Stamm at tackle, and end Bill Hall, as a nucleus, but everyone else was new. Speedy Dave Qualls could man the other end position. Two seniors, Jim Sullinger and Duke Bonnett, and junior Jeff Maher, had to fill the all-important interior of the line. Bonnett was a nasty blocker than no one wanted to face in Oklahoma drills, and Maher was a fireplug just built for guard, but Jim Sullinger was the question mark. He had played center since PeeWees, but he had no special talent other than extraordinary toughness. The lightest boy on the line, he had to come through if quarterback Allen Kot was to succeed.

Kot and Ruff were certainties in the backfield, but the rest of the running backs would be a rotating circus. Ozzie Pinson had been a star in the PeeWees, and Larry Steiner, despite a propensity to scamper around in the backfield for 15 seconds, darting from sideline to sideline in order to gain five yards past the line of scrimmage, would see a lot of playing time. The other running back, Arthur "Junie" Jones, was so bowlegged that he could straddle oncoming tacklers.

Leo was fielding a team with only one underclassman, but most of the seniors had never been starters. So when he told the *Record- Courier* before the season that "you can't lose 12 good boys to graduation and expect too much," he might have been telling the truth, although assistant coach John Lowry believed that in his heart of hearts, Leo thought he might pull one out of the hat.

Leo had to open the season in a strange position – facing a new team coached by his own former player. Field High School was a consolidation of Suffield and Brimfield, and was more than twice Windham's size. Their coach was Dale Kriz, whom Kot had coached over a decade earlier. And he had learned his lessons well, edging his old teacher 29-24.

Leo was furious. He had become enamored of the Oklahoma 4-4 defense of Bud Wilkinson, and had installed it in the preseason. Then it gave up 29 points in the first game, and Monday at practice Leo's first words were, "Hell's Bells, boys. We just can't run that 4-4!" He scrapped it on the spot, and went back to his standard 5-3 formation. He never blamed the players – he blamed himself for losing that game. That was Leo Kot. He was always a realist – he told his boys what to do, and gave them the opportunity to go out and do it, but if his plan was wrong, he took responsibility.

That 5-3 defense, featuring senior Jerry Downey and underclassmen like Pete Speicher, Lenny Kot, Bud Myers, Ron Nutter, and Rick Purdy in key positions, became the unsung wall that held opponents at bay, while the offense got all the glory.

And it WAS glorious. Just as in the season before, the Bombers began decimating the PCL. They finally beat Newton Falls. Danny Ruff scored five touchdowns against Rootstown. Four different players scored in a shutout of Randolph. A Crestwood team featuring future Pro Football Hall of Famer Jack Lambert fell 40-8. Streetsboro, in the middle of its first winning season, went down 18-12. As much as Danny Ruff was scoring, he was usually double teamed, so Steiner, Pinson, Qualls and Jones were also getting enough touches to frequently reach the end zone.

The team was almost giddy with its success. Playing for Leo was fun, but this was better than anyone expected. Nobody was going to stop the Bombers this year....

Or so they thought. Because the showdown for the county championship was looming on the field of Southeast High School, out on County Highway 18, the longest road trip of the year. Playing quarterback for Southeast was Larry Kehres, today famous as the coach with the highest career winning percentage in college history, at the University of Mount Union, but as a senior in high school, he was the hard-throwing successor to Aurora's Tom Curtis as the most feared passer in the league.

Leo prayed for rain – he actually said so in the game preview in the paper – but game day was bright and hot. And the game lived up to its billing. Kehres riddled the Windham defense with passes, but ultimately, it was three Bomber fumbles on the rock-hard, grassless surface that did them in.

That, and the officials. Danny Ruff erupted on one of his patented 54 yard breakaway runs, and six seconds later dropped the ball triumphantly in the end zone. But behind him, a yellow handkerchief fluttered to the ground. Dave Qualls, who was nearly as fast as Danny, ran convoy right behind him on the entire trip, and just as Ruff was about to cross the goal line, the last Southeast tackler, instead of heading for Danny, headed for Qualls. Right in front of the official, he ran in front of Qualls, and executed a flop worthy of any NBA player trying to fake a charge. It was obvious to everyone in the stands, but the clipping signal was the nail in the Bombers coffin.

So it was over again – doomed to yet another second place finish. Play out the schedule, turn in the equipment, watch basketball. Maybe even lose another game along the way. Aurora was coming to town, and they were as good as ever.

But Leo Kot wasn't going to let that happen. He never quit until the game was over. He might tell the paper that he "wasn't sure if his boys could get up for the Aurora game," but he practiced the team just as hard that week.

It paid off in the highest scoring game the Windham field had ever seen. Ozzie Pinson set a school record by running back two punts for touchdowns. Ruff, Junie Jones and Bill Hall each had a touchdown. Allen Kot even kicked the first field goal in school history. The Bombers won 36-22.

And then the impossible happened. Southeast lost to Kent State High School, 8-6.

Suddenly, the last game against the Garfield G-Men of Coach Gary Huber assumed monumental importance, because a win meant that the Bombers could claim a share of the Portage County League championship.

Leo was unusually quiet that week. Everybody knew the stakes, but the drilling was methodical. No changes, because both the offense and defense were in crackerjack shape. The variable was the weather. The headline in the Saturday morning edition of November 5, 1966 blared that a "Killer Storm Hits the Great Lakes." The sports section carried the story of Southeast's Friday night win over Rootstown. They had their share of the title. Now it was the Bombers' turn.

The weatherman wasn't wrong. By game time, the field resembled an arctic tundra, with six inches of snow covering the field. The players were half-frozen and completely miserable as they took the field.

Leo Kot brought out every trick he had learned in 17 years as the Bomber skipper. Knowing that Coach Huber had scouted Allen Kot's field goal the week before, he trotted his field goal unit out in the first quarter for a try on a stalled drive at the Garfield nine yard line. But Leo had no intention of trying a field goal in those condition. Allen snatched the ball from the holder and looked downfield where Danny Ruff stood alone in the end zone. The ball fluttered for a lifetime in the gale force winds, and settled into Ruff's hands for a first quarter lead. But the Bombers flubbed the extra point.

Ruff was also responsible for Garfield's first score, bobbling a punt at his own five. Two plays later Clark Kothera plunged over for a G-Men score. An extra point that split the uprights made the score 7-6.

It was a dispirited bunch of boys that Leo gathered in the dank, freezing locker room at halftime. Telling his assistants to wait outside, Leo herded the team toward the communal shower and told them to sit down. Speaking in a quiet voice, jutting out his lower jaw the way he always did when he wanted to make the point, he said only a few words.

"Boys, I've never asked you for much besides having fun and playing good football. But tonight, I want to ask you for something. This is my last game. I'm hanging up my jock. Do you think you could win this one for me?"

And then he walked out. No one said a word, because Leo Kot had suddenly forced 25 teenagers to become men. Our own physical misery didn't mean a thing now.

I won't pretend it was easy. Garfield wanted to win this rivalry game as much as we did. But as the third quarter drew to an end, Danny Ruff, playing the last game of his career, settled under a punt at his own 35, and slogging through calf-deep snow and every single player on the Garfield team, plowed his way 65 yards for a touchdown.

It held up. The Bombers won 13-7. They had won the PCL championship for their coach.

But no one celebrated on the way home, because Leo Kot was gone.

That 1966 Championship season was the high point in many lives, but thinking about it too much still causes grown men to tear up. Less than two years later, the real heart of the team, the boys who opened the holes for Ruff, Steiner and Pinson, guard Duke Bonnett and center Jim Sullinger, were dead, killed thousands of miles away in Vietnam. They've never been forgotten. In his very last interview, 17 years later, Leo said the 1966 team was his greatest moment in football, and he recalled Duke and Sully by name.

In a tribute article published the week after the Garfield game, Leo cited health reasons for his retirement. He was only 43, but he was already feeling the first effects of anemia, the disease that finally brought this giant down.

He still had almost 20 good years left in that fall of 1966. He stayed on as the Windham golf coach until his final retirement, even winning the PCL championship in 1980. He also returned as the head baseball coach from 1980-83. In 1971 he had come out of retirement to coach the freshman football team, a team with Hall of Famers Dave Flegal, Robbie Garrett, Jim Christopher, Barry Lyons, and a host of other great players who became Windham's first ever playoff team. Most people think that it was as much Leo's fundamentals as Stan Parrish's brilliance that got them there.

As Leo approached the end of his teaching career in 1983, he talked incessantly about retirement, how he'd hunt and fish just like back in Glen Robbins. And he'd spend his days golfing and bowling with his buddies.

The end came much sooner than anyone thought, only three years later. In his last days, as his former colleagues and players visited him in the hospital, I like to think he knew how much he had meant in all our lives. In that final 1983 interview, he said, "My career at Windham was definitely satisfying. If I had my life to live over, I wouldn't do a thing differently.

Many people who rubbed shoulders with Leo knew he had a wilder side, but there is so much to Leo Kot that it would take a full biography to cover it all. I talked to a lot of people about Leo in preparing this book, and almost every one of them choked up at some point in the interview, but I thought that Cliff McGuire, who was my teammate on that 1966 team, might have put it simply and best. He said, "You always knew that Leo was on your side, teaching you a few things and then pulling for you to do them right. And when you finally grew up, you could sit down with him, drink a beer, and talk to him as your friend."

Yep, that was Leo.

The Great Basketball Coaches
David Thomas

I hate basketball. I've hated it ever since tryouts for the seventh grade team. Coach John Lowry pushed a rack of basketballs at me. I thought he wanted me to show him the flashy hook shot I had developed in backyard games with Bob Chalker and Bruce Honobach. Instead, he told me he was glad I had showed up and thought I'd, and I remember his exact words, "make a darn fine manager." Damaged my psyche forever.

Now, I realize that hating basketball makes me a heretic in Windham, because Windham has had entire eras of basketball brilliance. Believe it or not, there was basketball before Marty Hill.

Boys basketball began in Windham in 1927. The new brick high school had just replaced the 1883 wooden building that sat where the student parking lot is located today. The white high school did not have a gymnasium, but the new one did. So when the Yellowjackets, the team nickname at the time, took the floor, they were playing in the most modern gym in the county – one on which the foul circles almost overlapped. And they were playing against Mantua Village, the defending county champions.

On December 19, 1927, in their very first game ever, the boys team, featuring Willis Belden at center and Bob Ehresman at guard, scored five points.

Mantua Village scored 92.

Almost a century later, it remains the most lopsided defeat in the history of Portage County.

The Windham boys basketball team did not win a single game for exactly four years. They lost 41 games in a row. So we have to start our search for greatness a bit later in time.

The 1930's were not a shining time for Windham sports, except for girls basketball, which dominated the county for the entire decade. The football teams were often so pathetic that they were disbanded before the end of the season. The basketball teams were a little better, but were seldom more than mediocre. No one foresaw things getting any better, until six-man football came to town in 1938.

Because that was the sport at which Windham would excel, becoming the Ohio state champions in 1939 and 1940, and international champions of 1940 when they defeated the best team in Canada. Finally, Windham had a crew of kids who were good athletes, and the winning spirit they fostered on the gridiron spilled over as those same kids donned their black and gold basketball uniforms.

The fall of 1939 was an uneasy time, both at home and abroad. Hitler's Nazi army had conquered Poland in October, the prelude to World War II. The *Ravenna Evening Record* headlined a story about a Randolph farmer whose pigs had trampled him to death in a feeding frenzy. James Naismith, the inventor of basketball, passed away. But Garrettsville High School had opened its shining new 42 by 65 foot basketball court, and the Windham boys, still glowing from their undefeated six-man football team, were ready to play for their new coach. His name was David Thomas.

A few older Windhamites might have bought insurance from Dave. At least some of them know that Dave was the husband of Katherine Thomas, the legendary teacher and principal after whom Windham named its elementary school. Over on the other side of the county, Dave is vaguely remembered as a quiet teacher at Southeast High School.

But very few people know that this mousy little math teacher was the first great boys basketball coach in Windham history.

He inherited from football coach Deane Eberwine a spectacular group of athletes, kids who would have been superstars in any era of Windham athletics. On December 13, 1939, against Nelson, he started Fred Stanley, Harold Stanley, and Bob Turner, each of whom would be first-team football All-Americans the next year. Completing the quintet were versatile Sam Scott and Ralph Drumheller, a bruising all-conference football player and the only senior starter. Backing them up were Robert Fechter, George Love, Kenny Nichols, Don Miller, and Robert McDivitt.

And despite being eager to translate their football success onto the hardwood, they lost three of their first five games, every one of them a Portage County Conference loss.

Maybe it was because they were playing for a new coach who had the position forced upon him. Corwin Gehrig, the previous coach, had moved on, and Superintendent Eberwine had few male faculty members on his staff. So a man who preferred working with numbers to coaching basketball players got the position by default.

And the very vocal Eberwine was hardly the role model for Dave Thomas to follow. Eberwine had taught his football players to fight back on the field. He frequently got angry and yelled at the boys. That was not Thomas's style. A very shy man, he didn't know how to raise his voice. In fact, Fred Stanley recalls that Dave was actually very polite when addressing his team, treating his players with deference.

But if he wasn't a rabblerouser, he did have a keen analytic mind, an abundance of patience, and an understanding of the fundamentals of basketball. Where Gehrig, a former football coach, had simply rolled the ball onto the practice court and had the players scrimmage, Thomas's philosophy was that organization would lead to success. He watched each player's style, figured out his weaknesses, and worked with him one-on-one. He would stay hours after practice, late into the evening, working with individuals on their shooting form and grounding them in the basics. He helped Fred Stanley develop a hook shot from the foul line that became a showstopper in those days of two-handed set shots.

This mild mannered man had decided that if he had to coach, he wanted the best team on the floor. He didn't care what year a boy was in school; if he was the best player, even a sophomore, he was in the game. Gradually, the players began to respond, and they also began to win. After losing to Streetsboro, Freedom and Hiram by a total of seven points, the boys entered January 1940 with something to prove. Thomas kept tinkering with his lineup, finally settling on Sam Scott at center, Harold Stanley and Nip Drumheller at forward, and Bob Turner at point guard, a continuation of his role as quarterback on the football team. Fred Stanley, although the tallest player on the team, was the other guard, so that he had room from which to launch that devastating hook shot.

Through January and early February, the wins began to come over teams that had feasted on them in previous years. They beat Mantua Village by 25 points, Shalersville by 14, Mantua Township by 24, Troy by 30, Garrettsville by 10. There were no superstars; Fred Stanley had the most points in any game, and that was only 12. By the end of the county regular season, they had a 5-3 league record, not spectacular, but solidly in the middle of the race.

But in 1940 the 19 team Portage County Conference had a league tournament at the end of the season to determine the 5 teams which would qualify for the "B", or small school, sectional tournament at Kent State University, played on an 84' by 50' court almost half again as big as Windham's gymnasium. Today every team in Ohio gets to play in sectional tournaments – not so 80 years ago. But the Bombers had to open against the Hiram Huskies, the regular season leader who had beaten them earlier in the season, on the first day of the tournament, which featured 8 games in 12 hours.

This time Coach Thomas emphasized defense, and his Bombers responded by giving up only seven field goals the entire game, not fouling anyone, and squeaking by, 18-15. This set up a quarter-finals game on a Thursday afternoon against Freedom, which had defeated Windham a month earlier. And if the Bombers won that game, they would have to play again the very same evening.

Once more Dave Thomas rejiggered his lineup. He moved Harold Stanley to center, Sam Scott to guard, and Fred Stanley to left forward, and Fred responded with his breakout game. Fred canned almost as many field goals himself, eight, as the entire Freedom squad made, and the Bombers won 34-23. After one hour rest, they again took the Kent State University floor against Edinburg, whom they had not played during the regular season.

Against the scrappy Scots, who did not have a single player taller than 5'8", Thomas again emphasized tight man to man defense, and this time his boys gave up only six field goals in four quarters. A 25-16 win sent them into the championship game against defending league champion Suffield, which had been crushing teams by a margin of 40 points in the tournament.

Oliver Wolcott, the longtime Ravenna newspaper sportswriter, said that Windham had been the "dark horse since the beginning of the tournament," which made the performance of the Bombers totally unexpected. Thomas sent his boys into a stalling game, completely nullifying the high powered Red Devil shooters and resulting in a lead of 4-1 at the end of the first quarter and 8-6 after the second. At halftime, Thomas told the boys to start feeding Fred Stanley under the basket, and guard Sam Scott made that his mission. Stanley scored nine points, the defense remained stifling, and at the end of the a 27-19 victory, the 1940 Bombers stood on top of the Portage County Conference with the first championship trophy that Windham's boys had ever won on a basketball court. And, equally important, they qualified for the sectional tournament for the very first time.

It was their misfortune to draw Waynesburg, a Stark County squad that had lost only two games the entire season, and one of those was to the defending state champion North Canton Vikings. The game was a classic struggle, and the teams were tied 26-26 with two minutes left. Waynesburg made the final two shots and left the floor as victors, the first step in what would eventually lead them into the state finals that year.

But Oliver Wolcott was duly impressed with the young Bombers. In his writeup of that game, Wolcott said that it was only due to playing on the larger Kent State court that tired Windham out – remember, they were playing their fifth game in six days on that full-sized court. He closed the article by saying that the success of the underrated Bombers was "due in no small part to Dave Thomas, their coach."

The months leading up to the following basketball season had to be the most exciting that the sleepy little town of Windham ever experienced. The Windham Bombers six-man football team returned from Niagara Falls Canada with an international championship to their name. The first draft numbers were drawn as American began its ramp-up for another world war. The federal government confiscated half of Windham Township, and the building of the Ravenna Arsenal became a 24 hour a day beehive.

Dave Thomas lost Nip Drumheller to graduation and Sam Scott to the armed services, but he still had the Stanley Boys and Bob Turner to build his squad around. Long distance shooter Bob Fechter, who replaced Scott, had been his sixth man the previous year, tiny Don Miller had been varsity the entire season, and he promoted football players Frank Janecek, Harold Belden, Con Thrasher and Bob Goss from the junior varsity team. He added the football team manager, Bob Pavlik, for good measure.

Oliver Wolcott wrote that Thomas would have to rely on "speed and clever ball handling," but did not feel that the team had the height to compete in the Portage County Conference this year.

The first game of the 1940-41 season was a road trip to Nelson, which had the most universally loathed gymnasium in the county. Nelson played on a floor in the white building that still sits on Nelson Circle. It had seating only on a balcony that overhung the court, making it impossible to shoot from anywhere but in front of the basket. But that didn't matter to Bob Fechter, who wore such thick glasses that he virtually had to smell the basket rather than see it. Fechter played the game of his life, draining eight long shots for 16 points in a 37-5 win that put the league on notice that the boys from Windham had found a second sport that they loved.

Fred Stanley scored only three goals against Nelson. So no one in the league knew the whirlwind that Dave Thomas was prepared to unleash: Fred Stanley had become a scoring machine.

The Bombers began a march through the county as devastating as Sherman had unleashed on Georgia. With Fred averaging over 20 points a game, unheard of in those days, and Thomas's stifling press often stealing the ball before the other team could reach half-court, the victory margins began to mount. Undefeated Streetsboro fell. Undefeated Hiram was next. When the Paris Night Riders came to town, featuring a junior gunner named Jim Purdy who would one day become the mayor of Windham, they were able to manage only seven measly points.

And still the Bombers rolled on. They whipped Mantua Township 51-14, with Fred scoring 34 points, a Windham scoring record that stood for over a decade. Aurora was shellacked 53-13. The other coaches around the league began to complain publicly that Dave Thomas and his boys were running up the scores to humiliate their opponents.

That was the last thing Dave Thomas would ever do, and the Ravenna newspaper even wrote an editorial telling the whiners how wrong they were. Oliver Wolcott compared Windham football mentor Deane Eberwine to Dave Thomas with these words: "Eberwine substitutes freely in his football games, but his boys are so good they can't help but score. Thomas has no good bench players, so he must keep his starters in." Reserves Bob Goss, Harold Belden, Art Joy, Frank Janecek and Don Miller must have cringed when they read this damnation with faint praise in the newspaper that day.

The Bombers clinched an undefeated regular season championship with a 50-21 win over Garrettsville. Fred Stanley scored 31 points, but the box score reveals that Coach Thomas played his second string for much of the game, perhaps responding to the public outcry, but at the same time showing that he did indeed have a depth to the team that no one knew about.

They needed it. The county tournament for the league trophy was next. Jim Purdy's Paris High School, still smarting from their earlier pasting, was the first opponent, and Fred Stanley had sprained his ankle. How good would the Bombers be without their superman?

Once again, as he had in the season opener against Nelson, near-sighted Bob Fechter picked up the slack. Raining impossible shots from all over the court, Fechter equaled his season best with 16 points. Frank Janecek filled in for the hobbled Stanley, giving him one day extra rest.

It wasn't enough. The Bombers next had to face Palmyra, a team they hadn't played in several years. The Redskins featured Bob Kehres, who a few years later would sire Larry, one of the greatest college football coaches in American history at the University of Mount Union. With Stanley dragging around the court in his lowest gear, Kehres put on a dazzling show of ballhawking and steals, and Palmyra pulled away after the first half to send the Bombers to their first defeat of the season, 24-18.

So they wouldn't defend their league championship this year, but the season wasn't over for Windham. They still had a chance to play into the sectionals, but they would have to win two consolation games on consecutive nights for that right. Fred Stanley was not going to allow a gimpy leg to end his career. Wincing every second of the game, Fred poured in 14 points to help beat Ravenna Township 28-10. In the consolation finals against the 14 and 1 Randolph Tigers, with Windham down 19-5 at the half, he scored 10 of his 15 points in the final quarter of a bitter contest to lead Windham to a 27-26 nailbiter. Oliver Wolcott was moved to call it one of the most courageous performances he had ever seen on a basketball court.

However, there was to be no fairy tale ending to this fantastic season. In the sectionals, the Bombers drew a Copley Indians team which sported an 18-3 record, and with Fred Stanley still not at full speed, the game wasn't even close. That 30-14 loss brought down the curtain on the career of one of the greatest athletes that Windham Ohio will ever see.

But Dave Thomas wasn't done. He might lose Fred Stanley the next year, but he had Fred's brother Harold, three year starter Bob Turner, and Con Thrasher, kid brother of female legend Charlotte Thrasher, back as starters. Art Joy and Bob Goss were now seasoned veterans, and Harold Belden and Frank Janecek were solid if not spectacular off the bench. They had to be – Thomas only carried seven players on the varsity that year.

With such a small number of varsity players, and without the monstrous presence of Fred Stanley in the middle, Thomas decided that a pesky defense would be the Windham trademark this season. In the season opener against Nelson, his boys gave up only three field goals the entire game. The scoring was spread out among Stanley, Thrasher and Joy in the 28-9 victory.

The boys did not have long to enjoy the win. The next day was December 7, 1941, the day the world changed in the air and waters of Pearl Harbor. The *Evening Record* suddenly became more interested in carrying lists of local boys fighting for their lives than in complete stories about high school basketball games. Before the Bombers played another game, war would be declared on both Germany and Japan.

As the Ravenna Arsenal began manufacturing bombs three shifts a day, Windham began to click off wins as methodically as they had the year before. Freedom and Streetsboro managed to score only 23 points between them in their losses. Mantua, Shalersville, and Braceville fell too, as Stanley, Joy and Thrasher traded top scoring honors nightly, and crowds began to fill the Windham gym to overflowing as people sought some relief from the stream of bad news coming from overseas.

Eventually, their very popularity cost the Bombers an undefeated season. On January 21, 1942, unbeaten Ravenna Township came in for a non-conference game. Windham jumped out to a 9-0 lead as fans continued to pour into the tiny gym, filling the stands, the stage, and finally onto the court itself. The officials had to continually stop the action to clear the floor, trying to push the crowd back. In the game-long confusion, Windham's press was frustrated by having to dodge bystanders. Ravenna Township used spectators as moving picks, and the Bulldogs' towering center, Bill Utterdyke, camped under the basket and pulled in lob passes for layups. Slowly Ravenna Township came back, took a 22-16 lead at the end of the third quarter, and withstood a furious Bomber charge at the end to win 26-25. Utterdyke had 16 of those points. It was the only regular season game Dave Thomas's boys would lose that year.

Three more wins over Garrettsville, Aurora and Mantua Township wrapped up Windham's second consecutive undefeated conference schedule. Again, the county tournament would be at Kent State University, and whoever won the conference trophy would have to win four games to claim it.

The Bombers opened with a rematch against Shalersville and came away with a 34-22 win. Three nights later, it was Streetsboro who fell 48-19 as Con Thrasher scored a season high 20 points. The semi-final against Randolph was a 36-14 laugher in which the Tigers scored in only two of the four quarters. Windham was in the finals, against Ravenna Township, the only team to beat them that season, and the Bulldogs were undefeated.

In his preview for that contest, Oliver Wolcott took time to pay tribute to a Windham player. He called Harold Stanley the finest schoolboy sportsman he had ever seen in his long sports writing career. Wolcott explained that in the tournament game with Streetsboro, fouls had reduced the Rockets to only four remaining players. Stanley, the Bomber team captain, called time out and sent Don Miller off the floor, so that both teams would have an equal number of players with which to finish the game. That was the effect that a coach like Dave Thomas could have on a team.

The actual game was everything that a championship game should be. Coach Thomas told the boys that the key to the game was shutting down Bill Utterdyke. They didn't – he still scored 14 points, but the tenacious defense of Bob Turner forced him out of the lane and he had to rely on his outside shooting. The scrappy, undersized Bombers shut down everybody else. No other Bulldog scored more than four points. Harold Stanley scored thirteen, Con Thrasher chipped in eight, and Art Joy had ten, including the last three baskets of the game, allowing Windham to claim its second Portage County Conference championship in three years, 33-27.

Only two days later, an exhausted Bomber squad returned to Kent to face off against Clinton, an equally tiny school on the border of Summit and Wayne Counties. After spending the entire season battling teams much taller than them, it must have been a relief to face a team of equal size. Unfortunately, Clinton featured two squat guards who were both among the top 10 scorers in the state that year. Between them they netted 32 of the 38 points Clinton scored that night, and despite 14 points by Harold Stanley in his final game, the Bombers fell 38-26.

And that ended the first great era of Windham basketball, two conference championships in an era when an undefeated regular season did not mean a trophy, in a league where 18 other teams had to fall before a champion was declared. No other Bomber team in the 1940's would ever scale the heights of those three teams of Coach Dave Thomas. As quietly as he had entered the basketball scene, Thomas left, turning the reins over to other coaches and going back to the math classes where he felt most comfortable. But he had established a legacy that would be reborn 10 years later.

The Greatest Basketball Coaches
Clayton West

By the end of the 1940's, Windham Ohio was the single most transformed town in the United States. Most noticeably, there were now over 3000 people in a village which had begun the decade with a mere 300. After dominating Portage County six-man football for nine years, Windham High School was shamed by a *Ravenna Record* editorial into dropping that sport and fielding an 11-man squad of embarrassing ineptitude. At the end of the decade, two new coaches rode into Windham, to alter its athletic landscape forever.

One of them was Leo Kot, who became one of the greatest football coaches in Portage County history.

The other one was Clayton West. If you've never heard of him, that's understandable. It was a long time ago. But what you need to realize is that Windham basketball would not be what it is today if Clayton West had not been here for a brief time 70 years ago.

Leo and Clayton both came from Kent State University. Leo was a football player whose career had been shortened by injuries. Clayton West was a star guard on the Golden Flashes basketball team. They may or may not have known each other at Kent State, but their arrival together created a symbiosis that elevated Windham back to the top of the Portage County League in both sports.

West had a short stint at Madison High School before he came to Windham to take over the basketball program of Gordon MacDonald. Legend has it that West was persona non grata in Madison – he had won a brand new Studebaker in a local lottery, and he took his shiny new car and his coaching ability out of town shortly afterward, leaving more than a few hard feelings behind.

Gordon MacDonald had been like Corwin Gehrig in the 1930's – roll the ball out and let the boys scrimmage. Clayton West's philosophy was Dave Thomas all over. West stressed fundamentals – he liked the zone defense more than Thomas's man to man – and he never met a fast break he didn't like. Of course, the game had changed enormously in the decade. The two-handed set shot was a fading memory, as numerous college and professional players abandoned it for the one- handed jump shot, so much harder to defend against.

Clayton West was still very much an athlete. Fred Stanley remembered playing golf with West in the early 1950's, and West literally ran from one shot to the next. Fred also remembers that West was a terrible golfer, so maybe he should have slowed down a little bit.

He motivated his players by jumping into the middle of a practice scrimmage and showing them what he wanted done by doing it himself. He brought in current and former players from Kent State University to practice with his boys, forcing them to a higher level of play than they could get by scrimmaging against the junior varsity team. And by the 1950-1951 season, he pushed the Windham Bombers to the top of Portage County basketball.

That team was blessed with a wealth of talent. Still playing in the old original 1927 gym, that team had seniors Jerry Nutter, Don Clark, Larry McManus, and Bill Balliette. Top notch juniors included Stan "Dodo" Permowicz, Clair Liddle, Richard Clark, and Bill Cunningham. And filling out the lineup was a gangling sophomore named Don Sampson, newly arrived in the housing projects and the tallest player Windham had ever seen.

Sampson was a pillar to build a team around, but he was still too wet around the ears to rely on, so West broke him into the lineup gradually. In the first game of the season against Aurora, he started Jake Nutter at center. By the third game Nutter had been shifted to guard, and Sampson took over the center spot, while West played with the rest of the lineup around him. Larry McManus, Dodo Permowicz and Don Clark got most of the minutes at forward. Short but dead-eyed Bill Balliette and Clair Liddle manned the guard positions. Every single one of them could score at any given moment – and boy, did they.

They opened the season on the road, blasting Aurora 92-42, setting a new school record for victory margin. It was a record that would be broken more than once in that very season. Jake Nutter exploded for 28 points, Don Clark had 18, and Larry McManus had 17. It looked like it was going to be a VERY good year. In the second game win over Garrettsville, Bill Balliette and Larry McManus together combined to outscore the G-Men. For the second week in a row, the box score looked more like a shopping list, as West rotated 11 different players into the game. And in the third game victory at Freedom, Balliette, Sampson, McManus and Nutter all scored in double figures. It was a pattern that persisted the entire season. Bill Balliette was usually the high scorer, but so many other players racked up significant points that it was hard to say that Balliette was the star of the team.

And then Clayton West did something that must have looked like madness at the time – in the middle of the week, he took his boys to Champion High School for a full-bore scrimmage.

Why in the world would he do this? Very simply – Champion had a bigger court, and West wanted to get his team ready to play the games that really counted, the games at Kent State University at the end of the season.

The boys thrived on it. They beat Hiram High School 82-29, shattering that ancient victory margin record they had established all of one month earlier. The next night, against the undefeated Atwater Spartans, they did it again, winning 85-29 despite West clearing the bench early in the game. Glenn Libis, the Atwater forward who was then leading the league in scoring, was held to 11 points despite having several relatively inexperienced second stringers guarding him during the game.

Wins over Southington and Randolph followed, and over Christmas break West had scheduled a non-conference holiday tournament as a moneymaker for the athletic department. He could not have known that Ravenna Township, Windham's old foe, would bring in an undefeated team. Or that Bill Balliette would choose that night to go 1 for 19 on field goals. The Bulldogs won 45-38, dashing the hopes for an undefeated season, but priming the pump for their February rematch that WOULD count toward the league championship.

But just as notable as the loss was the appearance of a new name in the lineup: Al Kinney, a tall, fast forward who was recovering from a football injury. And therein lies a tale. Kinney was a star running back on the football team, but he'd hurt his foot in a late season game. The assistant coach, who just happened to be Clayton West, assured him it was just a cramp, and began grinding the foot in a circular motion.

Clayton West was a great basketball coach, but he wasn't a doctor. Kinney's foot was broken, and Al's screams seemed to suggest that West's therapy really wasn't doing a lot of good.

Al was now healthy, but he wasn't just one more jock to squeeze into the lineup. Al Kinney was tall, 6'2', and could shoot the lights out in a gym. His playing time increased in wins over previously unbeaten Southeast, featuring Joe Kainrad, later to become a prominent Portage County jurist, and Rootstown. And Kinney really made the headlines when West moved him to center and he notched 23 points in a tough 60-49 win over Suffield. But everything that had come before was just a prelude to a January 14, 1951 rematch against Aurora. Now, Aurora wasn't very good. The Bombers had beaten them in the first game of the season, and to tell the truth, the Greenmen hadn't won a game in 3 years. So Coach West installed a revolving door of players, substituting almost from the initial whistle.

It wasn't enough. Seven Bombers scored in double figures, and Windham destroyed the Greenies 101-20, limiting them to six baskets. It's a victory margin that I doubt any Bombers team will ever exceed.

Maybe that win made the boys cocky. West had scheduled a late season independent game against much larger Chardon so his kids could get more experience on a bigger court. The Hilltoppers taught the Bombers a little humility with a 55-45 loss. Suitably sobered, they returned to face the meatgrinder part of their schedule, because for all their success, they were still part of a four-way tie for the league lead – and they had to play the other three co-leaders in just a two week span.

They had to travel to undefeated Garrettsville the very next night. The G-Men weren't intimidated, and by halftime led the Bombers by seven. Bill Balliette ignited in the second half, and Windham pulled out a 51-44 win. They needed the boost in confidence, because Mantua High School, the consolidation of the village and township schools, was coming to town, and the Red Devils wanted the league title for themselves.

Sportswriter Joe Miller called this a battle of three men, Larry McManus, Bill Balliette, and Al Kinney, against one, Mantua's enormous center Earl Wright. Red Devil coach Emil Wright fed the reporter the story that Wright had some kind of cooties, was sick with the flu and probably wouldn't play. He lied. And it took an unsung hero to save the Bombers that night.

Clair Liddle had been a starter all season, but he seldom scored more that a couple baskets. He wasn't exactly the team enforcer, but nobody pushed him around for rebounds. Liddle was a scientific player. During warmups, he'd watch where the player he was to guard liked to shoot from, and then during the game, that player would find Clair waiting for him at that spot. The other players loved him because his dad was Ed Liddle, the school custodian, who would do anything for Windham athletes, and frequently opened up the school at odd hours so the boys could sneak in for pickup games while the rest of the town slept.

That night against Mantua, Clair became the hero. While Mantua focused on stopping Kinney and Balliette, Liddle scooped up offensive rebounds like they were his favorite food and clanked them back in off the fan-shaped metal backboard. He scored only ten points, but they were the biggest baskets of his life as the Bombers won this battle of the unbeatens, 46-45.

Over the next few days, the early February temperature began to drop. On February 2 it bottomed out at 20 degrees below zero, the perfect setting for the hottest game in the county that year, the rematch between Windham and Ravenna Township. But for the first time that year, the Bombers were as cold as the ground outside. They made just 15 of 75 shots. Dick Stonemetz tallied 11 points in the last quarter to blow open a close contest, and the Bulldogs stymied the Bombers' hopes for clinching the league title 56-47. That loss dropped them back into a three-way tie with Ravenna Township and Mantua.

A 44-28 win over Southeast then set up one of the most thrilling finishes ever to a PCL season. County Superintendent Calvin Rausch decreed that a playoff must be held to decide the league champion. Lots were drawn, and Windham got the coveted bye into the championship game on Wednesday night against Mantua, which beat Ravenna Township to earn that spot.

West's boys were ready, sensitized by the one-point squeaker against Mantua earlier in the season. They knew were playing for a league title, but what they didn't know is that Don Sampson, the super sophomore, was not going to play. Jake Nutter, who had seen his playing time slip since Al Kinney's return, was going to have to pick up the slack.

He did. West moved Al Kinney out to guard, installed Nutter at center, and let him cram an entire season of glory into one game. 18 points later, Nutter had led the Bombers to a 62-55 win and its first PCL title since 1942. The boys posed for their championship picture, and Clayton West was shown once more in the only suit he owned – he really wasn't much for fashion. They didn't have much time to celebrate, because the county tournament to determine sectional qualifiers began the very next night.

It was a classic case of anti-climax. Playing lowly Rootstown, whom they had not faced in the regular season, Bill Cunningham was the only player in double figures. The Bombers scored only three points in the final quarter. Referee Tom Mariana said in the newspaper the next day that he had never seen a team go so cold so quickly. They lost 52-36.

So that loss meant Windham had to start the long grind back through the consolation games, four games in a single week. Re-energized by their mission, they swatted aside Hiram, Randolph and Suffield to make it to the finals – against Rootstown, which had fallen into the loser's bracket. The Bombers brought a 19 and 4 record in, but the Rovers weren't intimidated. They fell behind 42-27, and then a rerun of their first encounter began to play out. Windham went cold, Rootstown became red hot, and it took a last second basket by Bill Cunningham to pull out a 45-43 win.

Windham's 20 and 4 record gained them a high seed in the sectional tournament, and West jumped onto a 16 and 7 Hartville team that he thought was overrated. He ran the boys hard that week in practice – later in life, player Larry McManus thought perhaps too hard – and when they traveled to Kent State they were exhausted from the horrendous second half schedule they had played. Hartville turned out to be anything but mediocre. Neither the offense nor the defense clicked. Although West rotated players in and out trying to find a spark, only Al Kinney finished in double figures as Windham fell 55-48. It was a loss that Clayton West would not forget.

Jake Nutter, Bill Balliette, Larry McManus, and Don Clark were graduating. Clayton West would be going into the 1951-52 season with a half-empty tank. So if no one expected much from Windham that year, they wouldn't be blamed for the pessimism, which made Clayton West all the more determined.

As the new season began, the Korean War dominated the international headlines. The Cold War with Russia was one fallout from that conflict. The *Record-Courier* began running a bizarre weekly column entitled "How You Can Survive an Atomic Bomb." And Clayton West was going to make sure that Portage County knew his Bombers were coming. Only a blind person wouldn't know that it was the Windham Bombers who were in town: West's boys were the first team in the county to wear tight knit warmup uniforms before the game. He chose the color too: a dazzling banana yellow shade that became the envy of the rest of the league. He developed a new workout schedule, making the boys wear galoshes for running drills to make them light on their feet later in the season.

The Bombers that year featured seniors Al Kinney, Dick Clark, Stan Permowicz, Bill Cunningham, and Clair Liddle. Don Sampson returned for his junior year, and West added only three players from the JV's, junior Pat Strohm and seniors Dave Smith and Rich Brown. Two close wins over Garrettsville and Leavittsburg, and one easy win over Aurora, started the season, leading up to an early December match with Mantua, which had won the county tournament the year before. It wasn't even close, a 65-35 triumph for the Bombers. The next night an undersized Hiram team came to town, facing a Bomber squad with height on its side, since Permowicz, Kinney and Sampson were all over six feet tall. Kinney lit up the cords for 32 points, and every player on the team got in the scoring columns.

It would be a long time before they got to play again. Early season blizzards halted the basketball season for three long weeks. Senior Ceatta O'Sako, who later went on to a career in television, was able to get to the Prince of Peace oratory contest, where she won with a talk on "The Big Binge", but the basketball players couldn't take to the road in the sub-zero temperatures.

They finally got back into action in their annual holiday tournament. West had invited some big schools in to give his boys a test against much more physical players than the PCL offered. The opening game win against Madison became a literal slugfest as Permowicz, Dick Clark, Sampson, and Bill Cunningham were all sent to the bench with five fouls. Officials whistled a total of 60 fouls in the game. If West wanted physical, that's what he got. In the championship game, the Bombers thrashed Uniontown 66-45.

But Coach West wanted more. For his next game he brought in Middlebranch High School. It took a lot of Googling to find out where in the world Middlebranch was located, since it doesn't exist any more. Middlebranch today is known as Canton Glenoak, one of the biggest schools in the state. They had been state qualifiers the previous year. Coach wanted to test his Bombers against the best in Ohio, and his boys responded, blasting the Diamonds off the court 71-41.

The news of that win was swept off the sports pages by a frightening development in the housing project of Maple Grove Park, which was swept with a massive hepatitis outbreak. The county health department dispatched 30 Red Cross nurses, including local nurse Elizabeth Taft, to begin inoculating everyone in the housing projects, including team mainstay Don Sampson. The health commissioner blasted sanitation conditions, saying in the newspaper that "Many residents do not even have garbage cans. They set their garbage out in the open as targets for all the wild dogs in the area, of which there are many." 900 Windham elementary students were forced to line up for shots.

So it was good news when basketball resumed to drown out the embarrassment of those degrading daily announcements on the front page. Aurora and Garrettsville fell. Chardon came to town and the Bombers avenged the defeat of the previous year 59-49. Mantua received another thumping, longtime foe Ravenna Township was beaten by 14 points, and the next night, a tired team survived a scare by lowly Randolph.

The boys from a tiny Portage County town were beginning to be noticed around the state, because the Windham Bombers were now 15 and 0. Reporters began interviewing West about his players. They called Al Kinney "baby faced and rosy cheeked," although West tried to counter that by saying that "When Al goes up for a shot, something gives, and it isn't Al!" He also said that there were no *prima donnas* on the team because he wouldn't know how to coach one.

Bitter coaches at other PCL schools said that Windham was only good because of its small court, that they would get their comeuppance when they moved to the bigger floors. But what they didn't know was that once a week West was taking his boys over to Western Reserve Academy in Hudson to practice on its massive floor. He was running his boys through endurance cross-country training to condition them. And when he took his graduate classes at Kent State on Saturday mornings, he took several players with him so they could play pickup games on the very floor where the sectional tournament would be held.

Back in the league wars, the Bombers continued their inexorable march toward a title. They blasted Southeast 79-21, leading by 60 points at the end of the third quarter. In the final league game, they beat last year's nemesis Rootstown to win the regular season league title. The boys barely paid any attention to it. West had them focused on the next game, and then the next, and refused to let anything go to their heads. Braceville went down 79-36, and one more win against Atwater meant that Windham High School had finished the season at 18 and 0. And then the fun began.

Over 1500 people jammed Wills Gymnasium at Kent State to get a look at these boys in the bright yellow uniforms in their opening conference tournament win over the Hiram Huskies. Instead of relaxing before the next game, West loaded his boys onto a bus and took them over to Division A Howland High School to help them dedicate their brand new, regulation sized court. The Tigers came perilously close to ending the magical win streak, but Windham escaped with a 46-44 win. The very next night the Bombers were back in action in the county semi-finals, and West's conditioning regime paid off in a 72-33 win over Atwater to propel them into the finals against Rootstown.

West was confident. He even moved a jv player, Joel Harvey, onto the roster, and got him into the championship game. He played all eleven players that dressed for the game. He wanted them all to get experience on the big stage. And he threw a press onto the Rovers, causing their two big men to foul out before the end of the third quarter. The result was never in doubt, 61-37. The 1952 Bombers became the first PCL team in almost a decade to win both the regular season and conference titles.

They were now 23 and 0, and what West had been aiming for all year had arrived – the climb through sectional, district, and regionals to the state tournament. No Portage County team had been there since Garrettsville in 1932.

It was almost fated that Windham would draw Hartville, the very team that had knocked them out the year before. The game would be the first athletic contest played on Kent State's new floor. Wills Gym had been abandoned for the new Memorial Gymnasium, the same arena where the Golden Flashes still play.

The Bombers went into their stifling press from the opening tip, scarcely giving the Blue Streaks room to breathe. And they did that with panache, fouling Hartville only five times during the game. Al Kinney had 17 points, Dodo Permowicz had 15, and the Bombers became the first Portage County team to make the sectional finals in over a decade.

The next obstacle was Boston Local, today's Nordonia High School, which had destroyed North Canton in their opener. They featured three time Summit County All-Star Ed Kovach at center. Kovach was averaging 27 points per game, and West knew just who he wanted to guard him. He told Dodo Permowicz to forget about scoring, to make sure that Kovach had a headache all game long. Permowicz did his job well. Kovach had only one basket in the first half, only four in the second, and the Bombers waltzed to a 51-40 victory.

They were now 25 and 0. They were the first Windham team to make it to districts. And they were the only undefeated team left in the state of Ohio.

Obviously, the path was going to be tough. They drew Amherst High School, a completely unknown team. Amherst came from the west side of Cleveland, they had only won 11 of 19 games that season, but they were the smallest team in a conference of huge schools, and almost every one of their wins had been against Class A foes.

The Comets were not intimidated by facing an undefeated team - an undefeated team that had a lead at halftime. All they did was unleash Lee Bartlome, their towering ace shooter, who sank a 20 point barrage in the second half. Whether it was nerves on the big stage, or exhaustion, the Bombers lost their chance for immortality by making only 7 of 24 fouls shots. That was the difference. Their undefeated season evaporated in a 60-47 loss.

Many decades later, it's not quite so painful to look back at the way that season ended, and rather to glory in what those boys accomplished. 25 and 1! Was that the greatest Bomber team of all? I marvel at how Clayton West prepared his boys for the rigors of life. Dodo Permowicz went to Georgetown University and became Dr. Stan Permowicz, serving 41 years as a Navy physician. Bill Cunningham went to Ohio State and became an industrial engineer. Larry McManus, after being drafted into the Navy, became an accountant with a career as the vice president of finance at Trumbull Memorial Hospital. And Al Kinney, after teaching high school science in Windham, decided to become a professional musician, and became one of the most respected jazz and ragtime musicians in the country.

And they remained friends. Clayton West couldn't ask for a better legacy.

The Greatest Basketball Coaches
Dick Schlup

It didn't take long for larger schools to notice what Clayton West had accomplished at Windham, and they came calling with offers of more pay and better facilities. West moved first to Navarre High School in Stark County, and then Hubbard High School in Mahoning County, where he coached until 1979 and lived until he passed away in 2001.

Not that Windham didn't have facilities to match. In 1952, the Bombers got a brand new gym with a full sized basketball court. It's still the home of the modern day Bombers. Unfortunately, the basketball coach who replaced Clayton West, Lawrence Snyder, inherited a team depleted of height by graduation, and that miraculous 25 and 1 season was followed by a dismal 2 and 13 record. Snyder saw the handwriting on the wall, and the last Windham saw of him was a cloud of dust heading in the direction of Idaho. I'm willing to bet there were tar and feathers trailing after him.

So it was a good thing that Kent State University was still churning out young eager coaches, because that's how Dick Schlup showed up in 1953.

He started out slowly. The Bombers just barely improved to 5 and 13, followed by a 4 and 12 season. Maybe the players just weren't as talented – or maybe it was because Windham had been kicked out of the Portage County League and were the gypsies of the county, playing games wherever they could find them. Becoming an exempted village school was the cause of the banishment from the PCL into the wilderness of independent play. Some of the county teams continued to play the Bombers, but a large portion of the schedule was played against distant and obscure schools.

But in 1955 things began to change. Locally, the political buzz was that Bob Small was kicked off the village council because Mayor Paul Lisec decided that, since Bob was a public school teacher, he was ineligible to hold elected office. Council wasn't happy – after all, Bob was a popular and conscientious official – but when Solicitor Roger DiPaolo concurred with Lisec, they decided that if Bob had to go, so did DiPaolo, and he was unceremoniously fired too.

Dick Schlup had nursed his Bombers through those two abysmal seasons, and he felt that they had enough seasoning to be at least competitive this year. After all, he had seniors Ken Rowan, Doug Goodin, Don Wolforth, and Lefty Bowers, all with 3 years of his coaching. Sophomore Maurice Jackson would be back in January. Maurice had broken his wrist in the legendary football game against the so-called Warren Harding reserve team, when the defending state champion actually sent their varsity, featuring Paul Warfield, and went home embarrassed by the 7-6 loss to a school one-fifth their size. Juniors Don Gattrell, Dave Rininger, and Jerry Tacy moved up from the jv team, as did sophomores Gary Mizner and Wayne Hall. Not a bad team at all.

And then 6'2" Tom Denvir showed up. Denvir had been playing at Piketon High School down on the Scioto River. Tom's family left the year after a plant was built in Piketon that enriched uranium for atomic bombs. Maybe some of the radiation had affected Tom, because he brought a basketball talent that made Coach Schlup's eyes glow.

The season opened at home against Hiram on November 29, the very day that East Germany began building a wall through the heart of Berlin. Schlup expected to win that game, and his team didn't disappoint him. He was glad to get that initial win, because Southington was coming to town, and they were tough. They had a kid named Elmer Campanella, who had averaged over 20 points the year before.

Schup started a young lineup, with Doug Goodin and Lefty Bowers at guard, Denvir at center, and Ken Rowan and Wayne Hall at forward. For the first time ever, the Bombers had three boys over 6'2" on the floor at the same time. Rowan drew the assignment of guarding Campanella. Many later, Ken recalled that he did a decent job that night. He was not being modest. Campanella scored exactly no baskets that night, while Ken and Lefty pumped in 13 points apiece, the entire team shot 50% for the night, and the Bombers dumped the Wildcats 54-49. That's the night that Schlup decided he had something special in this group of kids.

Tom Denvir was a coach's dream. Schlup's boys ran a fast break any chance they got, but if the break wasn't there, Denvir would be, and before long his scoring average edged up toward 20 points per game. If Denvir had two men hanging on him, Rowan and Bowers took up the slack, both averaging well into double figures. Gary Mizner also began to see more playing time. Rootstown, Burton, Randolph, and Garrettsville all toppled before Christmas. Atwater, the defending PCL champs, took Windham into overtime, and it took 31 points from Denvir to pull it out. In fact, none of the games were blowouts, and Schlup sometimes put in Dave Rininger, a football player in short pants, to soften up particularly hot scorers on the other team.

But then, after Christmas vacation, the Bombers lost two straight games, one to undefeated Kent State High, by three points, and then to winless Twinsburg by two. Schlup had seen enough. He'd lost enough games the last two years, and he was sick of it. He began pushing his players in practice to be more aggressive. He'd jump into scrimmages, just as Clayton West had done, and bully the kids to toughen them up. He said that the zone defense was for "bloomer girls," his term for sissies, and that the Bombers would live or die with a man to man, glue-like press. For the rest of the season, Windham became the most frustrating opponent a team could face.

By then skinny Maurice Jackson was back, taking more and more of Doug Goodin's playing time despite still wearing a cast on his hand that resulted in a lopsided jumper. Jackson might have been the fastest kid who had ever worn the black and gold. Lefty Bowers was a good guard and a blistering shooter, but he was, well, left-handed, and left-handers are usually kind of goofy, according to athletic superstitions. So Maurice became the trigger man on the fast break, and suddenly, the games weren't close any more.

Schup used every man on his bench in a win over Western Reserve Academy, and the Bombers, behind Denvir's record-setting 38 points, still shot almost 60% for the game. The next night at Braceville, 12 boys got into a 25 point victory. Schlup wanted everybody on the team ready, because the next game was a rematch against Kent State High School. With Ken Rowan climbing all over Kent State star Jon Fenn, and Gary Mizner returning from a week of the flu, the Bombers got their revenge, knocking the Blue Devils from the ranks of the unbeaten.

Sophomore Wayne Hall began to assert himself in easy wins over Middlefield, Southeast, Crestwood, and Aurora, and suddenly the Bombers found themselves with a chance to earn a high seed at the sectional tournament, which was now being staged at the Canton Fieldhouse. One final blowout of Uniontown, where both Rowan and Denvir scored over 20 points and senior Whitey Kimmerling got into his only game of the year, meant that they had a 16 and 2 regular season record to present to the tournament committee.

No such luck. Once again, the curse of being an independent team rose up to bite them. The committee decided that "Windham would not be seeded because exempted village schools don't DESERVE a seed." Schlup was outraged, but there was no appeal. The Bombers would have to play their way through the entire tournament. And since they had such a cobbled-together schedule, they faced a two week layoff before their first game.

Schlup told a reporter that his boys were going to scrimmage some class A teams during the break. That was just a ruse. Instead, he took his team up to Hiram College and scrimmaged the Terriers as a tuneup.

First round foe Garrettsville presented no problem, losing by 30 points, but the decision by the tournament committee meant they had to face top-seeded Copley, and the Indians had knocked Windham out of the tournament the year before. Apparently the officials had been told that the Bombers did not belong there, and their whistles almost melted by the end of the game. Despite outscoring Copley from the field, Windham has hit with 28 fouls, and the Indians sank 19 of them to edge out the Bombers 53-48 on their way to a spot as regional runners-up.

Still, a final record of 17 and 3 was nothing to sneeze at, and although Schlup would have to replace two starters in Bowers and Rowan, he had an awfully good nucleus to build on in the late fall of 1956. In fact, he told the *Record-Courier* that "sure, we're going to be tough."

That's because he knew Denvir, Jackson and Hall were stars, Gary Mizner had grown three inches during the off-season and became an excellent replacement for Ken Rowan, and Don Gattrell, who had seen limited action the year before, stepped up as a replacement for Lefty Bowers. Jerry Tacy, Ned Hertzog, Ron Wirick and Larry Long were reliable seniors, so Schlup carried only three more underclassmen, juniors Bill Barker and Dale Kriz, and sophomore Bob Franklin.

As usual, they opened the season with a win against Hiram. Despite Windham shooting an ominous 5 for 20 at the foul line, Maurice Jackson showed that Denvir wasn't the only scoring threat Windham had, leading the team with 20 points. Schlup cleared his bench in the following 30 point rout of Rootstown, and followed that with a bizarre 62-19 whipping of Southington. The Southington coach had kicked his entire starting unit off the team for some unknown disciplinary infraction, so Schlup reciprocated by starting his second string. Undefeated Burton came to town, and they also got to see all of the Bomber players in a 25 point loss.

The gym was packed to overflowing for the next game, as two time defending PCL champion Atwater rolled into town, bent on avenging the overtime defeat of the previous year. Coach Jack Cordier had decided to play Windham's game. Two superb teams spent the entire game pressing without letup; neither team made a single substitution. Atwater won 49-42 – they would go on to be undefeated during the regular season – but the Bombers had nothing to be ashamed of.

Brushing aside Garrettsville, Windham entered unknown territory for their next game. Schlup had scheduled a contest against Youngstown Cardinal Mooney, a massive school several times the size of Windham. This was Mooney's first year of existence, but they were already 6 and 2, powered by a senior who had signed a letter of intent to play quarterback for Notre Dame. The Cardinals should have stayed home. The Bombers won 69-27, evidently unimpressed by the flamboyant style of the man who would become Ohio's most notorious congressman, Jim Traficant.

The next challenge was avenging that defeat the previous year to Twinsburg, and by this time Schlup's boys went on a rampage. Denvir and Mizner both netted 21 points in a 25 point win, and then it was clear sailing through the end of the season. Randolph, Ravenna Township, Braceville, and Kent State fell in quick succession. Against Randolph, Gattrell and Denvir outscored the entire Tiger team. Against Ravenna Township, it was Mizner and Jackson who accomplished that feat. The Bombers came close to 100 points for the first time in years in their 97-40 conquest of Middlefield, a night where they sank 41 of 90 shots. Even missing Tom Denvir, they beat another brand new school, Crestwood, as Bob Franklin stepped up to fill the void.

And then came a game for the ages, a game that should have been in the district finals: 13 and 1 Windham against 16 and 1 Boston Township. Schlup knew it would be tough when he booked it; the Bulldogs were led by John Jones, a varsity starter for four years who was leading Summit County in scoring with almost 30 points a game. Junior Gary Mizner played the game of his life, scoring 27 points. Jones was held to half his usual number of points, but a second quarter defensive collapse in which Boston scored 14 unanswered points proved too much to overcome, and the Bombers fell for the second time that year, 72-65.

The rest of the season would not be any easier. Southeast and Aurora fell without a fight, but Schlup, in his insistence on playing the best teams he could find to prepare for the tournaments, had scheduled another tough large parochial school, Warren St Mary's, for the final game of the season. Trailing the Mohawks by two points with 15 seconds to play, Maurice Jackson grabbed a jump ball and passed to Gary Mizner, who drove the lane to score and tie the game.

Except it didn't. The skimpy newspaper article simply states that "officials ruled that the goal didn't count." Maybe somebody who was there can explain it. All I know is that the Bombers ended the regular season at 15-3, and were once again denied a seed at the Canton Sectional, which is why they had to face 19-1 Brewster in the opener.

This time, however, Schlup's regimen of facing only the toughest teams all year paid off. Schlup figured their only chance was to slow the game down, since the Railroaders had been averaging almost 80 points a game. The only problem was that a stall game usually gives a team only outside shots, and the Bombers only made 20 field goals.

It was enough. In an epic game in which neither team led by more than three points until the final minute, and Tom Denvir was handcuffed by Brewster's 6'6" center, Maurice Jackson coolly scored 17, and the Bombers slipped by their first foe 49-44.

Next up was a familiar, dreaded opponent – undefeated Atwater. Schlup had learned from that earlier loss. He told his boys that he didn't want to see any daylight between them and the men they were guarding. And never was there a tighter defense – Atwater made exactly 11 of 61 shots that game. They didn't make a single basket in the first quarter. Tom Denvir couldn't move without a Spartan draped over him, but Don Gattrell collected 20 points to take the pressure off Denvir. It may have been the best game that Schlup ever coached, but he still resorted to an old coach's trick. A picture in the *Record-Courier* shows assistant coach Leo Kot calmly picking at his socks, while Schlup has his hands folded and his eyes rolled toward heaven. The score at the end was a divine 61 to 41.

Coming up was Doylestown in the first game of districts, a tournament only the 1952 Bombers had ever visited. Doylestown certainly had to be easier than Brewster and Atwater. After all, they had lost all of TWO games during the regular season. But Schlup believed that only the Bombers could beat the Bombers. And darned if they didn't try. First Tom Denvir fouled out. Then Wayne Hall followed him to the bench. Maurice Jackson picked up his fourth foul. Mizner, Gattrell and Franklin had three. The Chippewas spent most of the night at the foul line. But if they were at the foul line, that meant they weren't making field goals.

Maybe that's what Schlup had been praying for. The Bombers hung on for the win, 56-55.

So now they had gone further than any other Windham team in history. They'd knocked off three teams which had a combined three losses during the season. And all they had to do now was beat the Vienna Flyers, who had been in the state finals the year before. And Vienna's starting five averaged three inches taller than Tom Denvir.

The *Record-Courier* said the only chance the Bombers had were if they could bottle up the giants without fouling them. And they did, for 47 minutes and 58 seconds. With Windham leading 58-57, Ken Mishorich, Vienna's 6'5" center, drove the lane for a layup. Wayne Hall blocked him; it looked for all the world like a charge, but the referee didn't see it that way. The picture in the paper shows Tom Denvir forlornly holding the runner-up trophy.

Things would never be that good again for Dick Schlup.

He lost Tom Denvir and Don Gattrell, but he figured with Wayne Hall, Gary Mizner, and Maurice Jackson coming back, he'd be just fine. Bob Franklin had been a fantastic sixth man, and an amazing sophomore named Dave Flower was moving up from the JV team, destined to split a guard position with Bill Barker, a defensive wizard. Schlup thought this team could be his ticket to the state finals. He thought so even after losing Gary Mizner and Bob Franklin for part of the season with appendicitis, which seemed to have been contagious. And with only one single early season loss to Newton Falls, he just might have been right. A 17 and 1 record was great preparation for the Single A tournament in Canton.

Except Windham wasn't playing in the Single A tournament. Courtesy of a conniving villain from Mogadore named Ned Novell, described in the chapter on the Tomahawk Conference, Windham, for the only time in its 83 years of boys basketball, had to play in the big school tournament. Because of dropouts and transfers, Windham's enrollment was less than half that of their potential rivals. Wayne Hall tipped in a Maurice Jackson shot to beat Southeast in overtime in the tournament opener. Owing to the whims of an independent schedule, they still had to play one more regular season game, against Warren St Marys, and only Bill Barker's clutch baskets at the end pulled out a 68-67 win. In the AA division sectional finals against Springfield, Wayne Hall and Gary Mizner spent over half the game on the bench with fouls, but Schlup's boys still almost managed to pull it out, finally falling 61-57 to end another great season.

On August 8, 1958, Dick Schlup resigned. He never got to see the Bombers back in the small school tournament where they belonged. He was hired away by his alma mater, Kent State University, to become the head basketball, golf, and tennis coach at the brand new branch in Ashtabula. He brought Bill Barker and Maurice Jackson there to play for him the next year after they graduated, even letting the boys live with him for awhile. Tragically, his young wife died during a gall bladder operation, and that seemed to drain all his drive. He left coaching to become a college administrator, first in Ashtabula, and then in Lima when Kent established a branch there. And that's where the trail of Dick Schlup disappears.

So which was the greatest team in Windham's first 30 years of basketball? Was it Dave Thomas's 1942 team, featuring the same boys who had been international champions in six-man football? Or was it Clayton West's astounding 1952 team, that had the longest winning streak in the state of Ohio at 25 games? Or was it one of Dick Schlup's last teams, which lost only 6 regular season games in 3 years?

I think... the 1931 girl's team might have played any one of them to a tie. How's that for deferring until the second half?

Stan Parrish and the 1974 Windham Bombers Football Team

In the troubled days of 1974, as the United States endured a presidential scandal of unequaled squalor, a hyperactive head coach and a bunch of assistants barely out of college molded a bunch of local teenagers into high school Monsters of the Gridiron – arguably the best small school football team that Portage County has ever seen, before or since.

Leo Kot had retired after 17 years as head coach after that 1966 PCL championship. He was tired, and the first small hints of the anemia that would take his life 20 years later had already begun. He had shepherded his son Allen through high school, but Lenny, Kevin, Mike, and Billy would play under a different coach.

The natural choice was John Lowry, Leo's longtime top assistant and the yin to Leo's yang. For years they had played good cop/bad cop towards the players, but Lowry, whose stern military-bred demeanor belied an extraordinary skill as a teacher, inherited a group of underclassmen whose skill level was just a step below such stars as Danny Ruff, Tim Stamm, Duke Bonnett, and Jim Sullinger. The other PCL schools seemed to accelerate their talents, with Mogadore beginning its long string of league championships, and even perennial sad sacks like Kent State High School and Waterloo having one-year wonder teams.

John Lowry's teams won only eleven games in five years, and Superintendent Ken Jacobs, who had been a head coach at the old Palmyra High School during the six-man football era, and Principal Bob Wert decided that perhaps it was time for a change. Lowry, being a perceptive man, chose to resign before the hammer fell. They didn't have to look far for a replacement, because John Lowry, always a man of honor who demanded and gave respect, recommended one of his assistants for the job before he left for a new teaching and coaching position at Cortland Lakeview High School.

That assistant was Stan Parrish, and one would think that is where the story really begins. It doesn't.

Because during Lowry's last year as head coach, Leo Kot came out of retirement to coach the freshman team. He had his former All-Conference lineman Tim Stamm as his assistant. Stamm was a first year teacher good at carrying out Leo's plans, and there was nobody in the state of Ohio who could plan a team better than Leo. Leo had a team whose quarterback had won the F League state baseball championship as the rocket-armed catcher on Dick Viebranz's Globe Alloy Team. The winning pitcher on that F League team was now a fullback who could punish wimpy opponent freshmen as he ran play after play up the middle. Kot had linemen who were as big as the varsity players elsewhere.

Their names were Dave Flegal, Barry Lyons, Mike Hagans, Bill Rice, John Tresino, and Rob Garrett. They and their teammates were undefeated in that 1971 freshman football season, and THAT was the team that Leo Kot handed off to Stan Parrish, Windham's first year head coach. For the players, it began a three-year trek to high school immortality. And for Parrish, it was the start on the road to a Super Bowl ring.

Stan Parrish came to Windham not as a head football coach, but as a track coach. He graduated from Valley Forge High School in Parma Ohio in 1964, where he was an All-Conference running back. He then went to Heidelberg College in Tiffin, playing four years as a defensive back for the Student Princes. His Heidelberg coach found out through the grapevine that Windham High School had a job opening, and in July of 1969 Parrish sat down with Ken Jacobs and Bob Wert for an interview.

Like most teaching newcomers, he was immediately overloaded with job assignments. Not only was he teaching a full schedule, but he was also the head freshman football coach, the head eighth grade basketball coach, and the assistant track coach. Such is the life of a rookie in a tiny school district.

The next year all of his coaching assignments shifted. He took over as the head coach of the track team, and John Lowry elevated him to the defensive coordinator of the varsity football team. For the next two seasons, although the Bombers were less than overwhelming on the field, Parrish studied the Lowry method of coaching, and the biggest lesson he learned from John was to surround himself with capable assistants and to let them do their jobs. A lot of head coaches never learn to do that, which is why there are more ex-head coaches than active ones.

Then, in the spring of 1972, came that second sit-down with Jacobs, Wert, and Athletic Director Ed Permowicz, and Stan Parrish, four years removed from college, found himself the youngest head football coach in the Portage County League, taking over a team that had won less than half of their games the previous year – and that undefeated freshman team was still three years away from maturity.

1972 was a tumultuous year in America. The war in Vietnam, in which two linemen from the 1966 championship team, Duke Bonnett and Jim Sullinger, had been killed in action, still raged, tearing large holes between generations in this country. The Democrats had nominated George McGovern, a peace candidate, who had his own troubles when his vice-presidential choice, Tom Eagleton, resigned from the ticket after revelations that he had undergone electroshock therapy.

Stan Parrish had some personnel decision to agonize over. He was going to be a young coach leading a young team, one with only six seniors. He felt he was set on defense, with nine starters returning from Lowry's last team. The offensive line was the problem. Lack of size and inexperience could doom the team. Line coach Jim Burner would have his hands full.

But Parrish thought his backs and receivers could overcome that. Returning from Lowry's 1971 squad was Matt Myers, who might have been the most versatile athlete ever to wear a black and gold football uniform. He had started the previous season at split end, but was forced to take over the quarterback spot because of injuries. Now Parrish was going to move him to wide receiver. Bill Fugate was going to shift from tight end to fullback, to take advantage of his rugged blocking. Being plugged into the picture would be sophomores Dave Flegal at quarterback, Barry Lyons at end, and Rob Garrett at the other end.

Not for the first time nor the last, a first year coach forgot that reporters look for the big quote for their pre-season preview. And boy, did Stan Parrish toss them a softball. "I think we can win it all," he told the *Record-Courier* scribe. "Dave Flegal is going to pass the ball 40 times a game." Parrish was a coach with big league dreams, and it put a target right on the back of a bunch of rookies.

Windham had not scored against opening game foe Garfield the preceding two seasons. And in Stan Parrish's first game as a head coach, they made it three in a row. Dave Flegal passed 11 times, not 40, gave up two interceptions, and lost two fumbles. Welcome to the real world, Coach.

The second game against Streetsboro was a slight improvement, with the Bombers at least scoring in a 12-8 loss. For the third game, Parrish began experimenting, moving Matt Myers back to quarterback and Flegal to halfback, alternating them throughout the game. All this accomplished was a 4 for 15 passing performance between the two, and a 14-0 shutout by a previously winless Southeast team. Game four was against Mogadore, losers of their last nine games. Despite holding an 8-0 halftime lead, the Bombers once again fell 14-8.

The coaching staff was in a world of hurt. They knew the kids were playing their hearts out. So before the next game, against Rootstown, Parrish had a brainstorm. As he told the *Record-Courier* reporter, "I didn't go into the locker room before the game. I mean, how could I ask the kids to get up for the fifth straight game after losing the first four?"

Maybe his kids were happy not to see Stan before the game. Dave Flegal put the team on his back, completing 6 of 12 passes, rushing for 100 yards, scoring every single point, and the Bombers won their first game of the year 14-8. They might be one and four, but the season had turned around.

Andy Hedge became a stalwart at running back. Flegal was at quarterback to stay, and Barry Lyons had been installed at fullback, a position he would come to define. Lyons had been moved from tight end to fullback after bugging Parrish to let him carry the ball. Parrish tried him out in practice, and on his first run Lyons knocked out senior Bill Fugate, the starting fullback who was also a linebacker on defense. The fullback position became Lyons's by default for the rest of his career.

Although they lost the next game to Field, coached by Bomber alumnus Dale Kriz, an 8-0 score showed the defense had become the backbone of the team. Facing a game against out of league foe Leetonia, Andy Hedge erupted for the best night of his career, gaining 147 yards and leading Windham to a 22-8 win over the favored Bears. Maybe Parrish was right, and the Bombers would finish the season with at least a .500 record.

Of course, Parrish had not quite learned his lesson about restraint around reporters. Casting aside modesty, he said of his 2 and 5 team, "We should win the rest of our games now."

Nope. Didn't happen.

The big excitement the next week was President Richard Nixon, already under the cloud of a little affair called Watergate, stopping at the Isler farm in Windham Township to buy a pumpkin nearly as big as his head, and giving the cows on the Taft farm dysentery because they didn't get milked that day. Maybe Nixon should have stuck around to call some plays, as he supposedly did for the 1971 Washington Redskins, because the lowly Crestwood Red Devils broke a five-game losing streak that Friday, beating the Bombers 13-10 in a game so foggy the spectators could barely make out the action.

Coming to town were the Waterloo Vikings, whom Windham had never defeated. Stan Parrish was going to start nine sophomores on offense. One of them, Bill Roupe, notched the first rung on his ladder to stardom, catching his first touchdown pass of the year with less than three minutes to go to give the Bombers a 14-12 win to escape the basement of the eight-team Portage County League.

Parrish was ecstatic, crowing after the game, "If we win the next one, we'll finish at 4 and 6. I don't think that's a bad job." Why the reporter didn't mutter something about putting lipstick on a pig, I don't know.

But the sophomores did it. The beat non-conference foe Ledgemont by a score of 16-0. The two touchdowns were scored by Barry Lyons and Rob Garrett. The Bombers salvaged the shutout when hulking defensive lineman Bill Rice grabbed a tipped pass on the Windham two yard line and lumbered out to the 32 to end the game.

Stan Parrish ended his first year with an innocuous 4 and 6 record. He had three All-Conference players returning in Flegal, Lyons, and junior lineman Tom Liddle, whom Parrish at one point declared was the best athlete on the team. And the day after the season end, Parrish got to work getting ready in ways Windham had never seen before.

The daily news in 1973 could not have been more traumatic. The war in Vietnam had finally ended with the Paris Peace Accords, leaving five Windham boys dead in what many saw as a futile cause. Headlines called for the impeachment of Richard Nixon over the Watergate scandal and his refusal to turn over his office tapes, as demanded by the courts. Windham Council threatened the builders of the new homes on Belden Drive with a steep fine for building houses with no water shut-off valves. The fine was to be $1 a day.

A fight broke out at the 303 Club, 40 shots were fired, and Windham was placed under martial law for 24 hours in August. When school opened, 800 students were enrolled at Maple Grove School, leading to a panicked reshuffling of classrooms at both that school and East Elementary. The Booster Club built new stands on both sides of Ed Liddle Field.

Stan Parrish opened his second campaign with 20 returning lettermen, the most in the county, with only six seniors on the team. The *Record-Courier* called the first shot, stating that "The Bombers are rated by everyone as the team to beat in the PCL, although still a year from their peak." More prophetic words were never spoken.

The Bombers would start Flegal at quarterback, with Andy Hedge, Barry Lyons and Matt Myers, whom Parrish called "almost an assistant coach," as the running backs behind him. Two of the six seniors, Ken Dunn and Tom Liddle, were the rocks of the line, and slotted into the middle were juniors John Tresino and Mike Hagans, with Rob Garrett manning the tight end spot. A third senior, Espy Hedge, sustained an injury in the pre-season so severe he had to have surgery and wouldn't return until the end of the year. A sophomore, Jim Christopher, playing on a field named for his grandfather, was plugged into the line in Hedge's place.

Not only were they a year older, they were pounds of muscle heavier. The Windham weight program before that had used home-made weights that John Lowry had devised. After cafeteria boss Hazel Mallett had prepared her legendary Johnny Marzetti for school lunches, she gave the discarded tomato cans to Lowry, who filled them with cement and stuck a steel rod between them. Cheap, sometimes heavier on one end than the other, and not exactly the sort of thing you'd find anywhere but in Windham.

Parrish talked Ken Jacobs into buying a universal machine after the 1972 season. Parrish could be insistent, and Jacobs had a hard time saying no to someone whom he regarded almost as a protégé. The universal was installed in Oscar Tentler's old wood shop, and the boys spent the winter and spring in that cold, moldy annex. Long hours in the weight room created a camaraderie that Parrish hoped would translate to the field.

The season opened against defending league champion Garrettsville Garfield. Parrish had become a little more circumspect in his quotes, simply saying that "Garfield is the champ until somebody beats them." The *Record-Courier* reporter noted that he said it with a grin, and everyone knew that the unstated next line was "And we are that the ones to do it."

The coach was still smiling 24 hours later, as the Bombers staged a *coup d'etat* on last year's king, knocking off the reigning champ 20-8, and introducing the PCL to a primal force of nature. His name was Barry Lyons.

Frank Derry, the *Record-Courier* reporter, could not have been more awestruck, describing the systematic destruction of the G-Man defense by Lyons. Following an interception by Bill Roupe at the 46, Flegal sent Lyons plunging up the middle play after play, ripping off huge chunks of turf in an unstoppable march. Almost fumbling for adjectives, Derry alternated between calling Lyons "massive" and "mammoth" and "crushing" - words seldom used for running backs.

When he wasn't handing off to Lyons, Flegal was flinging the ball to fleet Matt Myers or running the ball himself. And in an ode to the unsung heroes on the line, Parrish said in his post-game interview, "We won the game with our linemen – our size just wore them down."

Against Streetsboro the next week, everything that went right against Garfield went horribly wrong. The defense gave up long pass completions. The offense fumbled the ball. And in a sign of immature players, four personal fouls kept moving the Bombers out of scoring range. The final score was 20-14 for Streetsboro in a game which Windham surely could have won.

The next week they whipped an inept Southeast team 24-0, but there were more ominous signs. The 24 points came on four touchdowns – the Bombers did not convert a single extra point. Dave Flegal scored three touchdowns, and he and Lyons rushed for 238 yards, but Flegal completed only one of his eight passing attempts. Once again, more penalties were called on Windham than Southeast.

Still, Southeast coach Marty Tausch said that the Bombers were, in his words, "One of the finest small school teams in the state." Parrish used those words as motivation the next week as they faced Mogadore, a team Parrish wrongly believed that Windham had never beaten, apparently not knowing that the 1957 Bombers of Leo Kot, featuring All-Stater Dave Flower and Hall of Famer Maurice Jackson, had spanked the Wildcats, the beginning of a 50-year feud between the two tiny schools.

The Mogadore game was an epic struggle, but the Wildcats were ready for Lyons. The Bombers were held to four yards rushing in the first half, and a disputed interception by Mogadore on a Flegal to Myers bomb left Mogadore on the up side of a 13-6 score.

Parrish was crushed. His post-game comment was that "for the first time since I came here, the boys did not give 100%." He must have realized how that comment sounded to the team, because four days later he had reversed his thinking completely. "We're disappointed," he said, "and we know the whole town is disappointed. We don't think we've been beaten by any team better than us. I have no one to blame but myself if we are not mentally ready to play football."

It got worse. The Bombers lost to Rootstown the following week 27-14, dropping their record to two and three. The season was starting to resemble a rerun of the previous year. Flegal was intercepted three times. The defense was dreadful, giving up 356 yards on the ground to a team which had only won a single game before then. The *Record-Courier* reported that Parrish moaned after the final gun, "This is a nightmare. I cannot believe what I'm seeing." Years later, Parrish said that this was the lowest he had ever felt in his young career; even a pep talk from Ken Jacobs couldn't raise him from his funk. Windham was an also-ran again, as it had been year after year.

The nation was preoccupied with the resignation of disgraced Vice-President Spiro Agnew that next week while Stan Parrish tried to regroup his demoralized young team. Undefeated Field was coming to town. Their coach, Dale Kriz, still harbored a grudge against his alma mater. Windham had beaten Field 14-12 in John Lowry's final season, on an 80 yard pass with no time showing on the clock, and the 8-0 win the previous year had not satisfied his desire for revenge.

In the weekly preview, Parrish praised Field to high heaven. He didn't want any locker room bulletin board material to make Kriz even more vengeful. Kriz countered with a sarcastic statement that since Windham had been the preseason favorites, the Bombers were the team to beat. All this was just psychological point-counter point, but Kriz meant for the Falcons to unload every weapon they had.

Kriz never called off his horses as Field methodically dismembered the Bombers 42-12, one of the worst defeats in Windham history. Parrish's terse post-game comment that "we got mauled" doesn't cover it. After the game, Principal Bob Wert went into the high school and took down the Class of 1956 picture hanging in the hallway. At least that's what he told the reporter. Field coach Dale Kriz graduated from Windham in 1956.

Stan Parrish must have seriously begun to doubt his coaching ability. It probably made him feel even worse to take a team of Windham cheerleaders to Garrettsville during the week for a Powderpuff game to raise money for new uniforms, and even THERE he couldn't get a win, settling for a 6-6 tie. Both teams made $140, and Buck Pelsue, the G-Girls advisor, got bowled over on the sidelines, giving him a stiff neck for the rest of his life.

Maybe that Powderpuff game wasn't really on Parrish's mind. The undefeated, state ranked East Canton Hornets were next on his table.

The score was 20-6. Windham didn't win. David Flegal had 30 tackles in that game. It didn't make any difference. This season was lost. The *Record-Courier* wasn't even sending reporters to Bombers games, depending on phone-in reports.

Despite the horrors of the last seven games, Parrish still believed in this team. Maybe a little tinkering would help. What he did, however, was insane. He took Dave Flegal out of the quarterback slot. Sophomore Kevin Kot took all the snaps the rest of the season, and he handed the ball off – to Dave Flegal.

It worked. With Flegal, Andy Hedge and Barry Lyons running the ball, the Bombers beat Crestwood 12-3. They beat winless Waterloo 8-0, gaining 180 rushing yards. And in the last game of the season, playing in a sea of mud and a blinding snowstorm, they intercepted four passes and beat Newton Falls 8-0. They scored exactly four touchdowns in three games, but they won them all.

The season from hell was over.

The day after Dave Flegal and Andy Hedge were named to the All-Conference team, Parrish began planning the next season. And this time, he had a real chip on his shoulder.

Jim Burner. Frank Omogrosso. Bob Leahy. Jim Rykaceski. Bruce Ribelin. And a baby faced rookie with a bad mustache, fresh out of Hiram College, named Marty Hill. Except for Windham legend Jim Burner, the glue to Windham athletics over half a century, Parrish assembled the youngest coaching staff in Portage County, and then had them pose for a group picture in coaching shorts which today would be called Daisy Dukes. He gave them each a job to do: build the best damned football team that Portage County had ever seen.

First, Parrish had to replace Matt Myers and Andy Hedge, tough to do with only one player, but he knew exactly who he wanted. Mike McCoy was the fastest kid in school, a free-spirited rebel without a cause who had quit the team in his sophomore year after a kerfuffle with coach Bruce Ribelin. He sat out his junior year, getting into trouble Windham-style. Parrish went to him and told him he was the piece he needed to complete the team. McCoy resisted, Parrish insisted, and to this day McCoy says that the persistent coach changed his life by refusing to take no for an answer.

Other holes were filled by kids with immense potential. Espy Hedge, Ken Dunn and Tom Liddle were gone, but coming up were strongmen Tom Denvir, as rugged an athlete as his dad had been 20 years earlier, Jim Christopher, with the fastest feet the coaches had ever seen in a lineman, and Dave Gearhart, the runt of the offensive line. And since both Gearhart and center John Tresino carried 4.0 grade point averages, the Bomber line could outsmart any dimwit who played over them.

Dave Sabula, Tim Hill, Mark Hedge, and Bill Roupe manned the defensive secondary. Roupe had the best hands on the team – he'd had key interceptions the year before and would have six more before the end of this season – and if any team got pass-happy, they'd have to get through them.

That's assuming they could get past the first two levels of Parrish's 4-4 defense. Rob Garrett, Tom Denvir, Jim Christopher, and Bill Rice, a backstreet brawler nearly as wide as he was tall but who had dropped 30 pounds of baby fat in the weight room, were nearly impregnable on the line. Gearhart, Flegal, Hagans and Lyons were probably the best linebacking corps in the state of Ohio on any level, including some small colleges.

Offensive line – check. Defense – check. And with a multiple offense featuring Lyons, McCoy and Tim Hill running the ball, and Flegal both running and tossing the ball to lightning-fast Bill Roupe, junior Hal Clark and Rob Garrett, Parrish thought his coaches had done what he told them – built the perfect high school football machine for a league in which they would play every single game against a school bigger than Windham. So he even scheduled a scrimmage against Ravenna, the biggest school in the county. That scrimmage got buried in the news that Richard Nixon had become the first president of the United States to ever resign the office.

The Windham band had 82 members that year, and Parrish had to roll his eyes when director Bonnie Furr cut into his pre-season practices. Furr had gone to the Board of Education and complained that the rotting band bleachers would put splinters in the bandsters' butts, to paraphrase her angry tirade, so a troupe of tradesmen cordoned off the end zone to prepare new quarters for those precious posteriors. And brand new lights had to be installed at Ed Liddle Field before the season began.

Back on the gridiron, in his preseason comments, Parrish wouldn't deny that the Bombers were the league favorites, but he told the *Record-Courier* that his boys had found the magic ingredient they had lacked the year before. "It's maturity," he said. "These boys have made up their minds that this will be Windham's year." The *Record-Courier* went out on a limb and predicted a possible football state playoff berth for Class A Windham – if they could knock off defending champ Field, the only Triple A (large school) team in the league, in the second week of the season.

So what was Parrish to do when, as Windham opened at home with Southeast, Barry Lyons got knocked out with a concussion, and Dave Flegal was ejected for an ill-timed punch at a Pirate cheap-shot artist? He went to the bench with a smile, putting in Kevin Kot at quarterback and Dave Sabula at running back. The Bombers amassed almost 400 yards in total offense, and they rolled to a 30-0 opening game win.

But they'd done that the year before, too. With Field coming to town, Stan Parrish would face the toughest test of his coaching life. Once again, Dale Kriz and Parrish played "You're better – No, YOU'RE better" in the press. Field had barely squeaked by Streetsboro in their opener, and maybe Kriz, for the first time in his life, really WAS worried. He should have been.

The game was an ugly classic. Parrish's post game comments summed it up: "That was sweet. We made a million mistakes and still blew them out of there. I've changed my philosophy. I used to yell at my kids when they fumbled. But now I realize that we are GOING to fumble. We play aggressive football, and as long as we do, we'll make some mistakes – and then make up for them."

The Bombers had beaten last year's champs 21-11, and not only had the team finally grown up – so had their coach. Windham rang up over 300 yards of offense, but Parrish simply said, "It was the defense who won the game. We turned off the best offense in the league."

Now, the season became a weekly game of King of the Hill. Every other team wanted the honor of knocking Windham down to size. New faces began to ring the field during those practices. Dozens of Ohio colleges sent scouts sniffing around Lyons, Garrett, Hagans, Christopher, and especially Dave Flegal. The *Record-Courier* hyperventilated with each new article about the team, and the coaches of upcoming foes began tearing their hair out.

The first year coach of the next opponent, undefeated Rootstown, pleaded "What will it take to stop Windham? A Mack Truck? The Hell's Angels? Yeh, that might do it. I sent my scouts to the Field game, and they thought the Browns-Bengals game had been switched to a Friday night. I kinda choked on my Coke when I heard that. They're at least two touchdowns better than any other team in the league."

Despite losing Tim Hill during the game, the Bombers won the battle of the unbeatens 12-7, although it took two fourth quarter fumble recoveries by Tom Denvir and a graceful Dave Flegal pass to Hal Clark in the end zone to cement the win. As Parrish said after the game, "The mark of a champion is to come back. Tonight, we had the poise when we needed it."

A fourth straight undefeated team was up next, arch-enemy and perennial league contender Garfield, and it will go into the record books as perhaps the greatest Bomber-G-Man game ever. Playing in a steady rain in Garrettsville, the Bombers left the field with a 14-12 win, and the *Record-Courier* reporter found Parrish slumped against a wall, almost at a loss for words, which NEVER happened with Stan.

"I'm shell-shocked. I'll never recover from this game. If you weren't here, you'd never believe it. It was like a high school Super Bowl. Whichever team had the ball last was going to win it."

Parrish was stunned because his vaunted offense was almost non-existent. The Garfield defense was ready for every weapon they had. The Bombers did not have a single first down in the first half. They only had two for the entire game. But the Windham defense rose to the occasion and bailed them out every time. Tom Denvir fumble recoveries and a blocked punt gave the Bombers the ball as the fourth quarter wound down. Bill Roupe pulled in 41 yard pass to set up a Barry Lyons plunge with a minute left on the clock, and after a three hour game, Stan Parrish's assistants almost had to carry him to the locker room.

But their reward came three days later. For the first time ever, the Windham Bombers cracked the top 20 in the UPI state poll. And even better, they were in first place in the playoff computer rankings, playoffs for which only four teams would qualify.

Winless Crestwood wasn't much of an obstacle, being held to minus 24 yards rushing and giving up two interceptions as the Bombers gave a 20-0 win to Homecoming Queen Laura Sabula. It was a good victory, despite Windham fumbling seven times, still a school record. Hapless Waterloo didn't stand a chance the next week, losing 33-0 in a Flegal/Lyons/Roupe/McCoy/ Mark Hedge onslaught.

Mogadore, which had six consecutive wins over Windham, was dismissed brutally when Barry Lyons went berserk, scoring 17 points, including one play in which he went over the end line with 11 Wildcats clinging to him, in a 29-0 thrashing that left Mogadore coach Norm Lingle dazed. "It was like standing in front of a freight train," he said, and Parrish didn't disagree. "That was one of the most awesome displays of offense I've ever seen. Our offensive line was outstanding."

Coach Jim Burner called the offensive line of Tresino, Hagans, Gearhart, Christopher, Garrett and Rice "the best I've ever seen at Windham, even better than when we were co-champs in 1966." That's the only quote for which my 1966 teammate Tim Stamm and I were never able to forgive our former coach.

Barry Lyons had now taken over the scoring lead in the PCL, and the UPI had started to really take notice, elevating the Bombers to sixth in the state poll.

After their 20-6 win over Streetsboro, in which the Rockets were so intent on stopping Lyons that Flegal completed 75% of his passes, the Bombers were the first undefeated PCL champions in a half a decade. For the first time in his career, the coach relaxed and waxed philosophic with the reporters as he clutched the game ball as if it was his first-born child: "When I took over three years ago, there were a lot of doubters that we'd ever win a title. Last year was a disaster, and this year could have been the same, except for the fact these kids worked so hard for this. We have some outstanding players, and some players who are maybe not so good, but every one of them has given me 120%. Every time we've had our backs against the wall, these kids have bounced right back."

So the PCL schedule was done, and the Bombers had two of their pre-season goals covered: to win the PCL, and to set a school record for wins in a season. Just one goal remained, 3 games away: the state playoffs.

Two more games, against Trumbull County teams, remained before them, bigger schools that could give them loads of computer points, but also a lot of trouble. The first one was against LaBrae, the Trumbull County League champions, and the Vikings had just been upset by Newton Falls, who would be the Bombers' final opponent.

The perfect season vanished at Ed Liddle Field that Friday in a battle of the titans, as the team fought to an 8-8 tie with LaBrae. They were lucky to escape with that, scoring only when Tim Hill took a punt on his own 16 and proceeded to run into his own blockers. As Hill remembered it, "I was going down and Ed Hinkle grabbed my jersey and pulled me upright again." 84 yards later, Hill hit the end zone with Windham's only TD of the night. It took a fourth quarter safety by tacklers Denvir and Garrett to nail down the tie.

But the tie gave them the computer points to earn the second spot in the computer rankings behind defending state champion Middletown Fenwick. Just get through the Newton Falls game in one piece, hopefully with a win to make it an undefeated season, and then the Bombers were going where no Portage County team had ever been before: the playoffs, the Final Four in the state of Ohio.

Once again, the defense rose to the challenge after repeated special teams errors, like muffed punts on the eight yard line. As Parrish said after the 14-2 win over the Tigers, "I told you in August that defense was the name of the game. When Jimmy Christopher picked up that fumble and ran 40 yards with it to end the game, that proved it."

As soon as the state announced that Windham would be playing parochial school Fremont St. Joseph at wind-swept Donnell Stadium in Findlay, 150 miles from Windham, the longest trip any playoff team had to make, Claire Liddle began selling tickets for a chartered fan bus at his barber shop on North Main Street. The Bombers were the only public school in the playoffs. They carried a lot of dreams, and 60 years of Windham football history, on their teenage shoulders.

During their week of preparation, the *Record-Courier* announced that a stunning seven Bombers had made First Team All-PCL: Garrett, Tresino, Rice, Hagans, Christopher and Lyons, and David Flegal made history by being chosen first team on BOTH offense and defense. Another five, Roupe, Clark, Gearhart, McCoy and Mark Hedge, made the runner-up team. The Bombers finished fifth in the final UPI rankings. Dave Flegal was chosen the defensive player of the year in Ohio by the Associated Press.

The papers buzzed with preview articles touting St Joseph running back Joe Guyer, who had averaged nearly 200 rushing yards per game. Stan Parrish and his coaches had scouted St Joseph, and they thought their boys were ready for them.

There were tons of distractions through the week. Parrish had to go to Columbus to get the game tickets. The *Warren Tribune Chronicle*, which usually treated Windham like an unwashed step-child, sent out photographers that interrupted practice.

Superintendent Ken Jacobs and Athletic Diredtor Ed Permowicz weren't going to let the team travel on regular school buses. They rented the most modern commercial buses they could get on short notice, using travel expenses the state supplied. Win or lose, they wouldn't have to trek home in the middle of the night after the game; they were going to stay in a Findlay hotel.

So on Friday, November 15, 1974, after a breakfast at the school, the Windham Bombers got the send-off they deserved. The police and fire department led the buses on a lap through the streets of the town, sirens blaring. Every player on the team remembers it to this day.

Parrish set the mood on the trip out to Findlay. "You're representing your town and Portage County tonight. This is history – you're the first to ever do this. I want you to play your hearts out, but whatever happens, you'll remember this for the rest of your lives."

The one thing Parrish couldn't prepare them for was the intense cold, an arctic refrigerator in those days before every player wore gloves and Under Armour could make a freezer seem cozy.

It was a battle in the trenches. The Bombers had prepared for Guyer, but the Crimson Streaks were equally prepared for Barry Lyons. In the first half, Fremont ran 32 plays to only 16 for Windham. On that frozen tundra, Fremont quarterback Greg Kuns completed only one pass all night, but it was for a touchdown, something that would be very dear that evening. Despite two blocked punts by Rob Garrett, the Bombers just couldn't get moving. Maybe it was because iron man Mike Hagans got knocked out of the game with a concussion.

Completely shut down by the slanting Fremont defense that seemed to play right into Windham's rushing tendencies, Flegal got Windham's only first down of the evening on a gorgeous pass to Bill Roupe, who flew to the Fremont seven – only to be hauled down from behind, something his teammates have jokingly never let him forget. The Bombers could not punch it in, and that's where the game ended, a 6-0 loss.

After the game, Flegal, who had every right to be sad after such a tragic loss, showed the maturity to put the game in perspective. He understood that the backs got all the glory, but it took a whole team to get them there. "It sure wasn't the line's fault," he said. "They've done one heck of a job all year. We wouldn't have been here without them."

The *Beacon Journal* and *Record-Courier* both carried game coverage articles. The *Record-Courier*, though, had a bonus article following the game stats.

It talked about how Stan Parrish had resigned as the Windham head coach after the game.

As shocking as it was, his resignation was a late season decision, one that he was going to make no matter how far Windham went in the playoffs. Purdue University had been pursuing Barry Lyons, and in conversations with their recruiter, Parrish picked up on hints that if Barry came to West Lafayette, Indiana, there might be a graduate assistantship in it for his coach.

Parrish was a professional coach. He had always aspired to go as far as he could in his chosen field. He'd been at Windham six years, still coaching track, still coaching eighth grade basketball in addition to being football coach. It was time for him to move onward and upward, taking the 1967 Windham Homecoming Queen, Ruth Purdy, with him as a bride.

It was a course that would take him all over the United States. After Purdue, he moved on to Wabash College, where he led the Division III Little Giants to an incredible 42-3 record, earning a spot in the Wabash Hall of Fame. After another stop at Purdue as an assistant coach, he went on to head coaching positions at Marshall University, where he had the first winning season in 20 years, and Kansas State.

Five years as an assistant at Rutgers in New Jersey landed him a coveted position at the University of Michigan, where he mentored quarterbacks Brian Griese, Drew Henson, and Tom Brady. His success there took him to the pinnacle of coaching, the National Football League, where he won his Super Bowl ring with the Tampa Bay Buccaneers. The man who once thought the Windham-Garfield game was a Super Bowl had actually arrived there.

After Tampa Bay came five years at Ball State University in Muncie Indiana, including two years as head coach. And in 2010, he claimed to leave coaching for good, except that a coach never REALLY gets football out of his blood. He volunteered as a coach for the Siena Heights Saints in Adrian Michigan, a tiny college which fielded its first team ever the year he arrived. And that position led him back to major college football, as he became the offensive coordinator for Eastern Michigan University, even serving as the interim head coach during the 2013 season.

And he still loves Windham Ohio, and those boys who gave 120% for him.

After Parrish left Windham, some of the coaching staff stayed with new head coach Barry Schaad, who eventually became a principal at Little Miami High School in southern Ohio. Most of them stayed in coaching with various degrees of success. Jim Rykaceski became a school superintendent in Grafton Ohio, and Bruce Ribelin is a long-time Portage County political leader. Bob Leahy followed Barry Schaad south and still coaches high school basketball. Even Marty Hill accomplished a few things by staying in Windham for four decades.

After that 1974 season, the boys drifted away to other things. Some disappeared without a single trace. Some stayed in town, like Tom Liddle, Hal Clark, Tom Denvir, Ed Hinkle, Rob Garrett, and Dave Gearhart, who helped prepare the Bombers of tomorrow as coordinator of the youth football league.

Center John Tresino is a pharmacist in Findlay, where he played his last high school game. Tim Hill married Homecoming Queen Laura Sabula and lives in Fairmont West Virginia, where he's been a sales rep for John Deere for over 30 years. His brother Jody, the skinniest 6'5" fullback you could ever see, who was Windham's very first first-team All-Stater in basketball, is an ordained minister in Deerfield. Mike McCoy has worked for Diebold in Canton his entire life, and is in charge of their education division, teaching 5000 people a year about the ATM software for their machines.

Some of the boys went on to play some college ball. Bill Rice played for one year at Youngstown before transferring to Kent State to get his degree in chemistry. He has spent the rest of his life working in laboratories, currently for the Erico Company in Solon. Bill Roupe played some college ball at Heidelberg, and Mike Hagans played at Heidelberg too, before he began a career in coaching and teaching that brought him back to Windham for a few seasons, and to Garfield as their head coach and athletic director.

Barry Lyons took Stan Parrish with him to Purdue, and after coming home began a career in law enforcement, starting as a Windham cop. He's still at it as a detective for the Portage County Sheriff's Department.

Rob Garrett was one of several Bomber players who ended up on the University of Akron team. Dave Flegal also starred for the Zips for four years. He eventually joined Parrish on his staff at both Marshall and Kansas State before returning to Ohio for a high school coaching and athletic director career. Dave is still active as a coach on the Revere High School staff.

And Jim Christopher, a year behind his fellow linemen, also played four years for the University of Akron. He coached at Akron after he graduated, then moved on to become the head coach at North Union High School in Richwood, Ohio in 1984. In November 1987, just after the end of the football season, he developed a pulmonary embolism and suddenly, tragically, passed away. He never got to see his son Andrew graduate from the United States Naval Academy in Annapolis, and enter training as a pilot.

Several other teammates also died much too young. Mark Hedge, that hard-nosed little running back, Dave Denvir, Dave Graham, Ken McLean, and Dennis Dean have also passed away over the years.

Coach Jim Burner, the quintessential Windham Bomber who played for Leo Kot in the 1950's and never took off the black and gold, passed away after a short battle with cancer. Somewhere, he's still coaching.

When I first announced my research into Stan Parrish and his championship team, I received emails saying the 1953 team was better, or that the 1986 PCL champs were just as good. Maybe. I have my own prejudice about the 1966 PCL champs. But until someone proves differently, those 1974 boys are the best that ever wore the Black and Gold, the greatest of the first half-century.

Acknowledgements

The book would not have been possible without the assistance of many people and institutions which shared their knowledge with me over the years. Some of them are no longer with us, but their contributions will never be forgotten.

Overarching support came from the Kent State University Library, especially its Microfilm Archives. Newspapers consulted every step of the way included the *Ravenna-Kent Record-Courier*, the *Akron Beacon Journal*, and the *Warren Tribune Chronicle*. I'm forever indebted to the Windham Exempted Village Schools and the Windham Historical Society. Two people who encouraged my historical research were Huber King and Lynnea St. John. The man who whetted my interest in written historical research is my high school teacher and coach, John Lowry, who never thought that our daily classroom battles would have such a profound effect.

Important information for the chapter on Girls Basketball came from June Millard Brobst, Violet Wilson Carr, Marie Miller Dutter, Grace Shively Ehresman, Gladys Snyder Farrington, Corrine Comyns Kotkowski, and Hazel Schwenk Wellman – all of whom were basketball players between 1928 and 1940. Invaluable information about the legendary Young girls who played for Raymond Hilty came from descendent Thomas Jacoby.

First hand memories of the two Six-Man Football eras came from Fred Stanley, the oldest surviving player from the Deane Eberwine era, and his teammates Don Miller and Robert Goss. Belvira Smith Angle, one of the six-man cheerleaders, delighted me with a unique perspective on the trip to Niagara Falls, and cheerleader Nickey Alger Dalzell wrote me about her memories of the last years of six-man football, sending along pictures used in this book. My best information about Eberwine himself came from his granddaughter, Jeannie Lawson. Many memorable hours were spent talking with and viewing the scrapbooks of Lois Mulally Turner, the sister of players Bob and Paul Turner. Jan Janecek Okeson, daughter of player Frank Janecek, graciously shared many pictures and articles collected by her father. Information about the war years of Six-Man football were furnished by Matt Myers, the son of Izzy Myers, and players Bill Alger and Van Simpson. And my most intimate connection to the Six-Man era is the scrapbook collection of my father, Harold Belden, who as a student journalist not only played in but also reported about the games. My brother David Belden had preserved these until it was time to share them in this book.

Having played for Leo Kot, I wanted to pay tribute to him for years, but many people helped me understand much more about the man. Absolutely the most indispensable aid came from Leo's son Dr. Lenny Kot, who lent me Leo's wartime diary, the family's most precious possession, as well as filling in gaps of Leo's chronology. Intimate knowledge of Leo came from his assistant coaches John Lowry and Oscar Tentler. Some of the most nostalgic interviews I conducted were with some of Leo's earliest players: Norm Clark, Stan Gill, Al Kinney, and Ed Ryan. And helping to jog my memory of Leo's final years as the Bombers' head coach were my teammates Tim Stamm (who remembers every play of every one of his games), Roger Stier and Cliff McGuire. It was my joy to interview the person who knew Leo the best, his older brother Tom Kot, who remained the biggest booster of Kent State athletics until the day he passed away.

Restoring the legacy of the Tomahawk Conference brings me great pride, but I could not have done so without the input of Tomahawk athletes Bill Barker, Jim Burner, Buz Davis, Joe Fabry, John Freudiger, Rich Gorby, Barry Hertzog, Bill Isler, Larry Minter, Chuck Schimmel, Ron Slagle, and Gary Wolfgang. Ron Ehresman, while not an athlete, furnished enthusiastic memories of that era as he encouraged my endeavors.

I met many basketball players from the different eras about which I have written, but I drew heavily on the memories of Bill Cunningham, Al Kinney, Coach Harry Kraft, Larry McManus, Stan Permowicz, Ken Rowan, and Fred Stanley.

Head Coach Stan Parrish talked with me for hours about the 1974 Bombers, but I was also able to recall that magic year with Pam Christopher Cree, Dave Flegal, Mike Hagans, Jody Hill, Coach Marty Hill, Tim Hill, Barry Lyons, Coach John Lowry, Mike McCoy, Coach Frank Omogrosso, Coach Bruce Ribelin, and Principal Bob Wert.

Special thanks go to Robin Martin, who has acted as my Boswell for many years, volunteering to videotape my talks for posterity, Sam Folmar and David Belden, who acted as sounding boards for my protean writing style, and Helena Belden, for the best 50 years of my life.

Illustration 1: Windham's first girls basketball team. Coach Ray Hilty wears his Bluffton letter sweater. Holding the ball is future Hall of Famer Gladys Snyder Farrington.

Illustration 2: The final girls basketball team. Front Row: Margaret Norton, Beulah Smith, Francis Beckinbach, Charlotte Thrasher, Hazel Schwenk, Joyce Janecek. Back Row: Belvira Smith, Hazel Lutz, Emily Grondeski, Iona Chaffee, Corinne Comyns.

Illustration 3: The 1940 International Champion Windham Bombers. Front Row: Frank Janecek, Harold Belden, Harold Stanley, Fred Stanley, Bob Turner, Joe Pinney, George Brauker. Back Row: Robert Fechter, Conrad Thrasher, Bill Richardson, Sam Scott, Don Miller, Art Joy, Bob Goss. Back Row: Manager Robert Pavlick, Coach Deane Eberwine.

Illustration 4: The 1941 Six-Man football team on original field, showing present day Bauer Avenue in the background.

Illustration 5: The 1946 Windham Bombers six-man Portage County Conference champions. This squad was so overpowering that the Evening Record castigated them for still playing six-man. Windham returned to eleven-man the following year. Left-handed passer Bob Garrett is number 2 on the right; his receivers were Izzy Myers, number 12 on the left, and Buffer Smith, number 5 standing. Coach Gordon McDonald is on the right.

Illustration 6: The 1945 cheerleaders for six-man football: Left to right, Peggy Chambers, Nickey Alger, Laurel Ball and Betty Bertram. Each graduating class contributed one girl to the squad.

Illustration 7: Legendary Windham Coach Leo Kot during his playing days at Kent State University.

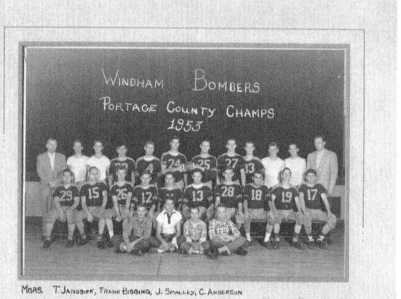

Illustration 8: *Leo Kot's first PCL champs, who played every single game on the road.*

BACK ROW, left to right: Managers, C. Pierce, P. Diroll, T. Minter. SECOND ROW, left to right: Assistant Coach, H. Kraft, A. Nichols, R. Stanley, J. Rininger, J. Lutz, R. Minter, C. Grafton, C. Kane, J. McCleary, C. Schimmel. THIRD ROW: Head Coach, L. Kot, J. Fabry, T. Turner, B. Warner, J. Mansfield, L. Delong, J. McDaniel, L. Minter, R. Bushey, S. Everhart, E. Berrington, Trainer. FOURTH ROW: J. Erbe, C. Chase, J. Steiner, R. Stanley, J. Burner, F. Cassetto, T. McCleary, G. Wolfgang, J. Moore, J. Goss.

Illustration 9: The 1960 Bombers, Tomahawk Conference football champions. The league disbanded the following spring. Windham won every football trophy during the three years of the Tomahawk's existence.

L. to R., TOP ROW: L. Kot (Coach), J. Kline, B. Higgins, B. Hertzog, Mgr. J. Miller.
SECOND ROW: Mgr. P. Diroll, L. Minter, A. Nichols, R. Minter, L. Hicks.
THIRD ROW: C. Chase, O. Booher, C. Schimmel, L. Nutter, P. Clark, R. Bushey, J. Freudiger.

Illustration 10: The 1961 Bombers, runners-up in the state championship game, and the last Tomahawk team ever.

Illustration 11: The 1961 team captains, Buz Davis and Jim Burner, with Coaches Harry Kraft and Leo Kot.

This page intentionally left blank in memory of all the Bombers athletes who are no longer with us.

Illustration 12: Leo Kot in his role as driver training teacher to several generations of Windham teenagers.

Illustration 13: Coach Dave Thomas and his 1941-42 Portage County Conference champions, first ever for the boys teams.

Illustration 14: Coach Clayton West and his 1951-1952 Bombers, who had a 25-0 record before falling in the tournaments.

Illustration 15: Hall of Famer Don Sampson sinks a layup in 1951.

Illustration 16: Dick Schlup and the 1957-58 Bombers. Dave Flower, #8, and Maurice Jackson, #5, are members of the Hall of Fame. #14, Bill Barker, became the youngest mayor in Windham and Ohio history.

Happiness Is Being A Bomber

1966 Portage County League Co-Champs

ROW 1 - A. Jones, D. Qualls, K. Bonnett, J. Downey, J. Sullinger, B. Hall, A. Kot, G. Belden, T. Stamm, O. Pinson. ROW 2 - L. Steiner, D. Ruff, R. Miller, L. Kot, D. Miller, G. Lewis, D. Dunavant, R. Starkey, P. Snyder, J. Lewis, M. May. ROW 3 - P. Speicher, T. Hedge, R. Nutter, R. Purdy, N. Myers, J. Maher, B. Held, R. Hurd, C. McGuire, ROW 4 - Coach Kot, Mr. Lowry, J. Hankins, J. Riggs, T. McManus, E. Welcome, M. Purdy, Mr. Burner, Mr. Jordan. ROW 5 - managers D. Hardy, G. Coz, A. Speicher.

Illustration 17: Leo Kot's last team, the 1966 PCL Co-Champions

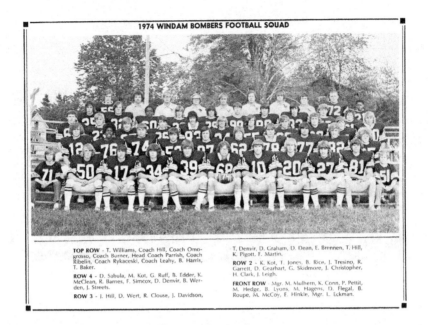

Illustration 18: *The first Portage County team to make the state football playoffs.*

Illustration 19: Coach Stan Parrish is carried off the field after the 1974 Bombers won the PCL championship

George Belden graduated from Windham High School in 1967, where he played football, wrestled, and ran track. He received his B.A. from Hiram College and his M.A. from Kent State University. He taught English for 30 years at Maple Heights High School, where he coached football, and was the head coach for both volleyball and golf. He taught British Literature, Studies in Popular Culture, The Literature of Sports, and Television Journalism. He has never lived outside of Portage County. He still owns his Windham letter jacket and intends to be buried in it.

Made in the USA
Columbia, SC
30 June 2018